AU

Contemporary
sociology of
the school
General editor
JOHN EGGLESTON

The ecology
of the school

CONTEMPORARY SOCIOLOGY
OF THE SCHOOL

PAUL BELLABY
The sociology of comprehensive schooling

BRIAN DAVIES
Social control and education

SARA DELAMONT
Interaction in the classroom

JOHN EGGLESTON
The ecology of the school

ERIC HOYLE
School organization and administration

COLIN LACEY
The socialization of teachers

PETER MUSGRAVE
The moral curriculum: a sociological analysis

PHILIP ROBINSON
Education and poverty

MICHAEL STUBBS
Language, schools and classrooms

WILLIAM TYLER
The sociology of educational inequality

TOM WHITESIDE
The sociology of educational innovation

JOHN EGGLESTON

The ecology of the school

METHUEN

First published in 1977 by Methuen & Co Ltd
11 New Fetter Lane, London EC4P 4EE
© 1977 John Eggleston
Printed in Great Britain
by Richard Clay (The Chaucer Press) Ltd
Bungay, Suffolk

ISBN (hardbound) 0 416 82900 7
ISBN (paperback) 0 416 82910 4

CONTENTS

CONTENTS

Prologue

Two roads diverged in a wood and I –
I took the one less travelled by –
And that made all the difference.

Robert Frost
The Road not Taken

Acknowledgements

The writing of this book has been illuminated by many experiences. I have played a part in determining the ecology of education in my work in schools, colleges and universities as a governor of schools and colleges, as a member of a local education authority and as a member of a number of national bodies involved in the distribution of educational resources. I owe much understanding to these experiences and the conversations with colleagues that have enlivened them. I must make it clear, of course, that the ideas and opinions that follow are my own not those of the bodies and individuals with which I am associated. Even though ecology presupposes a shared environment it is unquestionably an environment that is individually interpreted.

I must also record my appreciation of the work of Mary McBratney and Barbara Wiggins in preparing the manuscript and the assistance of the Keele Institute of Education Library in tracking down much elusive material. The Athlone Press of the University of London has kindly allowed me to use some of the ideas and a diagram from my chapter in Baron and Taylor's collection of papers entitled *Educational Administration and the Social Sciences*, and Philip Robinson has kindly allowed me to delve into his collection of statistics.

John Eggleston

Editor's introduction

Sociology has changed dramatically in the past decade. Sociologists have provided an ever-increasing diversity of empirical and theoretical approaches that are advancing our understanding of the complexities of societies and their educational arrangements. It is now possible to see the over-simplification of the earlier sociological view of the world running smoothly with agreed norms of behaviour, with institutions and individuals performing functions that maintained society and where even conflict was restricted to 'agreed' areas. This normative view of society with its functionalist and conflict theories has now been augmented by a range of interpretative approaches in which the realities of human interaction have been explored by phenomenologists, ethnomethodologists and other reflexive theorists. Together they have emphasized the part that individual perceptions play in determining social reality and have challenged many of the characteristics of society that earlier the sociologists had assumed to be 'given'.

The new approaches have had striking effects upon the sociology of the school. Earlier work was characterized by a range of incompletely examined assumptions about such matters as ability, opportunity and social class. Sociologists asked how working-class children could achieve in the schools like middle-class children. Now they also ask how a social system defines class, opportunities and achievement. Such concepts and many others such as subjects, the curriculum and even schools themselves are seen to be products of the social system in which they exist. In this study of the school we can see with special clarity the ways in which individual teachers' and students' definitions of the situation help to determine its social arrangements; how perceptions of achievement can not only define achievement but also identify those who achieve; how expectations about schooling can determine the nature and evaluation of schools.

This series of volumes explores the main areas of the sociology of the school in which new understanding of events is now available. Each introduces the reader to the new interpretations, juxtaposes them against the longer standing perspectives and reappraises the contemporary practice of education and its consequences.

In each specialist authors develop their own analyses of central issues such as poverty, opportunity, comprehensive schooling, the language and interaction of the classroom, the teacher's role, the ecology of education, and ways in which education acts as an instrument of social control. The broad spectrum of themes and treatments is closely interrelated; it is offered to all who seek new illumination on the practice of education and to those who wish to know how contemporary sociological theory can be applied to educational issues.

Schools are a human artefact – for the most part a very recent one. Yet their variety appears to be endless – new forms appear with ever-increasing speed. In consequence, even within a single educational system – such as that of England and Wales – the nature of the schooling available to a child can be dramatically different. Between different local education authorities and even between neighbouring residential areas the differences between educational 'climate' can be striking. Such differences are not only in the system or organization of schools or in the availability of buildings, teachers and resources, but also in the 'ideology' of the local education authority and its various schools and the regimes to which this gives rise. This book considers some of the evidence of such macro- and micro-differences and some of the political, social and economic environmental factors that may account for their distribution – uneven and at times apparently sporadic.

But it is not only the incidence of distribution that is interesting. Even more remarkable are the unmistakable consequences it has upon the opportunities, experiences, expectations and achievements of children and their teachers. After many years of exploration of the consequences of social class and community differences we are now beginning to see that the kind of schooling provided – its organizational structure, its buildings, staffing and other resources – may itself be an important factor in determining what happens to children.

There are many clues that point to this area of investigation and a substantial body of evidence exists that can illuminate our examination of them. This book presents the striking evidence of the uneven distribution of school provision and resources that has been assembled not only in surveys and reports but also in case study evidence. It also considers the wide ranging and important analyses of these differences. Evidence on the consequences of differences in schooling is examined in the light of the debate on the efficiency of strategies of intervention and 'resource engineering'. Developments such as the Educational Priority Areas and similar strategies of differential enrichment are considered in an attempt to answer the question: 'To what extent can planned modification of the ecology of schooling bring about real changes?'

Particular attention is paid to the process of distribution and the complex interactions through which this process is played – both at the macro- and the micro-level. But above all the book considers the evidence of the ecological variables and the administrative, political and ideological consequences that spring from them.

John Eggleston

1

The case for an ecological study of education

A major part of the study of education is the search for an explanation of its differing responses and outcomes. Why do some students achieve at such markedly different levels from those of others? Why does schooling appear to lead to high adult status for some and the converse for others? Teachers, administrators and researchers have regularly focused their inquiries on the pursuit of the elusive factors that may explain these and a thousand other differences that recur daily in the life of schools and classrooms. The history of education is strewn with accounts of key variables which were believed to embody the explanation of differential educational performance. They have included divine intervention, the inner nature of man, heredity, intelligence, social class, the imperatives of the economic structure and the differential 'constructions of reality' of individuals.

The ecological approach offers the prospect of yet a further explanatory factor which has a compelling, even obvious, attraction. It is one that embraces and augments rather than supplants most others. It springs from the basic understanding that human beings take on different patterns of behaviour and different life styles and accept different patterns of achievement when they find themselves in different locations. And at any moment in time these locations are given and unchangeable; there is no choice but to accept them. It is important to recognize that it is not just the physical geographical aspects of location that are significant here but also their economic, political and social characteristics. For example, the ecology of power in a society or community has profound effects upon all who find themselves in that environment, not least of all on those who work in schools.

It is argued in this volume that there is a 'natural' habitat in which human beings live and respond. It is, like all other habitats, a created environment. It consists of a wide range of institutions such as homes, factories, offices, churches, cinemas and bingo halls. One of the most important features of the human habitat is the school – an inescapable part of the environment of all individuals for some of the most formative years of their lives.

Ecological study is not just concerned with the response of individuals to their environment. It is also concerned with the creation, maintenance and distribution of the resources, human and material, that constitute the environment. In its educational aspects it is concerned not only with the response to schools but also with the demand for the provision of schooling. In education the diversity of provision is often a more visible feature of the environment than the distribution of response. Certainly the variety of education systems and their schools, curricula and personnel appears to be endless; moreover, new forms seem to arise with ever-increasing frequency. Even within a single educational system the types of resources available to one child often appear to be dramatically different from those available to another.

The ecological approach

How may we consider this bewildering variety of educational provisions and responses? To an unaccustomed observer the scene is rather like an ant heap, a confused mass of apparently unrelated and unpatterned activity. Yet careful and sensitive observation reveals regularities of behaviour that imply shared understandings and recurring sequences. In making such studies the biologist and natural historian engages in the study of *ecology* which is characteristically concerned with the behaviours and life styles of organisms and their relationships with their environment.

Human beings, like all other living organisms, have a capacity to survive – to feed, grow, repair and reproduce by using and adapting to their environment. However, their life not only depends on taking from the environment but also on contributing to it. It is a two way process that is essential both for the survival of the individual and of the environment. Biologists have frequently alluded to the complex balance of inputs and outputs that maintains the soil, air, water, temperature and light in the correct conditions necessary to sustain a particular combination of organisms that need precisely those conditions.

It is this interaction that is at the heart of the study of *human ecology*. As in 'biological' ecology the focus of study is on the ecosystem in which the living organism and its environment survive. It is within the ecosystem that we can obtain a total picture of the twin features of stability and change. All organisms and all environments attempt to restore disturbances to the ecosystem; all attempt to minimize the effect of unavoidable disturbances.

Biological use of the concept of ecology takes two forms – *autoecology*, the study of relationships between individual living organisms and their environments, and *synecology*, the study of relationships between living groups and their environments. Human ecology is particularly concerned with the latter form and has tended to examine the relationship between human groups and their physical environment, looking particularly at their occupation of domestic, community and work locations. Quinn (1964) has suggested four main areas in which social scientists have developed ecological orientations – descriptive studies, physical environment explanations, ecological interaction and the study of human adjustment to physical environment.

It is from this last form, attributed to Hawley (1950), that much of the present enthusiasm for ecological study arises. In the popular literature of environmentalism and conservation the imperatives of man's ecological environment are emphasized and the urgency of man's need to adjust to his situation is proclaimed. A typical example is Meadows *et al.*, *The Limits to Growth* (1972), which suggests that such adjustment is essential if human society as we know it is to survive beyond the next hundred years.

It is clear from such studies that the use of contemporary human ecological approaches is far removed from the role of a convenient scientific concept; it has developed powerful ideological overtones. Lowe and Worboys (1975) in an illuminating study, *Ecology and Ideology*, write:

17

The lesson of 'ecology', in its broadest sense, is supposedly harmony, balance and symbiosis. As in technocracy where politics as traditionally understood is deemed to be redundant through the overriding and deterministic effects of man's technological situation, so in environmentalist writings political differences are declared equally redundant because of the 'imperatives' of man's ecological situation. Compelling physical and natural constraints supersede and replace moral and political imperatives; the new social order being of necessity subject to 'ecological determinism'. In Britain, recurrent calls for an ecological party indicate the presumption that environmental issues transcend orthodox political alignments.

They go on to quote McHale (1971):

Though seemingly innocuous in its theoretical origins, ecology generates a radical view of human society which may prove to be more 'positively' revolutionary ... than any of the socio-political ideologies which have previously challenged our traditional economic and institutional arrangements.

Resource management

A central instrument of this new radical view of human society is resource management. O'Riordan (1971) writes:

Resource management is a more comprehensive and positive term than conservation, and may be defined as a process of decision making whereby resources are allocated over space and time according to the needs, aspirations and desires of man within the framework of his technological inventiveness, his political and social institutions, and his legal and administrative arrangements. Resource management should be visualized as a conscious process of decision involving judgement, preference, and commitment, whereby certain desired resource outputs are sought from certain perceived resource combinations through the choice among various managerial, technical and administrative alternatives. Resource management involves strategies of action involving computations of tactics and methods and a variety of objectives. The emphasis is upon flexibility and the minimization of long-term environmental catastrophes, while maximizing net social welfare over time. The allocation process is dominated neither by the market place nor by the quasi-political forum, but by a combination of social, cultural, economic, and institutional processes that strive for the best solution, but which inevitably must seek compromise.

Clearly such ambitious claims for control and the bid to establish ecology as a major branch of science that is linked with them are likely to be contested. Lowe and Worboys (1975) review the essentially political debate that has emerged, particularly over the 'doomsday' threat used by ecologists to support their arguments. They conclude, 'Seen in these terms, ecological environmentalism represents a deeply conservative response to a moral crisis in Western society', and remind us of Ashby's assertion: 'The danger is political, not ecological, collapse.'

The ecological map

In this volume we shall not be initially concerned with the political or ideological implications of the 'ecology movement', though the debate will inevitably constitute a continuing backcloth to the discussion, and the consequences for education will be considered in the final chapter. We shall begin with a detailed description of the distribution of resources in which the evidence of wide variations and unevenness combine to produce an 'ecological map' of the very greatest interest.

The ecology of education even more than the ecology of 'nature' is an ecology of shortage, even scarcity, of resources. Even in periods which, with hindsight, seem abundant there are clear and visible limits to the enrichment of the environment. But though the concept of limits is common throughout ecology, not only the possibility but also the inevitability of human intervention appears to be far greater in human ecology. Certainly it is widely believed that it is this intervention that is responsible, more than any other factor, for the unevenness of educational resources that causes so much interest and feeling in modern societies.

The degree of interest and concern is hardly surprising in view of the massive size of public spending on education. Even a single local education authority (London) spends over £200 million each year and almost all spend over £3 million a year. The education service is now one of the country's largest employees and largest property owners and takes a major share of the products from a large section of manufacturing industry – notably the building, printing and furniture trades. It constitutes in total one of the really 'big spenders' of contemporary society. Yet, despite the magnitude of the education industry, 'we face a pervasive ignorance about the production function of education – that is, the relationship between school inputs, on the one hand, and school output as conventionally measured by achievement scores, on the other' (Blaug, 1970).

For this reason a central task of the book will also be to consider the differential *response to* educational provision; as we have already indicated, this has been the mainstream application of ecological study in education and a considerable range of data is available for discussion. The conflicting conclusions reached by Coleman (1966) and Jencks (1972) using the same overlapping data banks illuminate the considerable problems of ecological analysis and the particular difficulty of identifying causal factors. The book will draw attention to the hazards, not always fully recognized, of diagnosing causality from correlations and the use of statistical aggregates to summate individual behaviour. It will be argued that the development of proper caution is an essential stage in forwarding the understanding of ecological factors.

This will be followed by a consideration of the evidence of the process of distribution in which the complex interrelationship of supply and demand of educational resources takes place in a social, political and economic process. Important evidence of the process can be obtained from a number of case studies of educational administration and also from the examination of pressure groups. Here we shall also consider the attempts to bring about changes in the distribution of resources through strategies of intervention and resource engineering. These may be strategies which attempt to redistribute the allocation of resources, such as the Educational Priority Area programmes, or the access to resources, such as the comprehensive reorganization of secondary schools, or the attempts to rationalize the entry to higher education currently being attemped in several European educational systems as described, for example, in Crauzaz's *Diversification of Tertiary Education* (1974) and in *Contours of a Future Education System in the Netherlands* (Dutch Ministry of Education and Science, 1975). It is essential, however, to distinguish the two concepts of compensatory education. One, embraced by the Plowden Committee and many others, sees resource engineering as a mechanism of compensating for personal and domestic 'inadequacies'. This concept has been widely criticized by Bernstein and others:

> The concept 'compensatory education' seeks to direct attention away from the internal organization and educational context of the school, and focus attention upon the families and children. The concept 'compensatory education' implies that something is lacking in the family and so in the child. As a result, the children are unable to benefit from schools. It follows then that the school has to 'compensate' for something which is missing in the family, and the children are regarded as deficit systems. (Bernstein, 1970)

The other concept more appropriate to this book, is that of resource redistribution to compensate for resource deficiency. It sees resource distribution and usage as an important area of consideration in its own right with implications that transcend the limited focus of social deficit.

The micro-ecology of education

The ecological approach is by no means confined to macro-analyses. Much ecological study has been focused on the ways in which small groups respond to their immediate physical environment – particularly their architectural environment. Writers with architectural training or orientations such as Nicholson (1972) and Gould (1976) have already attempted to apply such analyses to education. The impact of such views is unmistakable in many schools – the brightly painted and decorated walls, the carpeted floors and the open plan layout. As with the macro-ecological approaches it is easy to overemphasize the strength of environmental forces and to reach a fallacious position of physical determinism (Broady, 1967). Yet it is equally unmistakable that the environment of learning is not devoid of significance. And as Richardson (1967) has demonstrated, the significant micro-ecological environment is by no means a solely physical one. Like the macro-environment, it is composed of social, economic, political and ideological components.

The book concludes by returning centrally to the ideological issues that are built into the ecological distribution of educational resources and the ecological distribution of response to them. The ecological mapping of the book will provide data for the consideration of the important consequences that spring from the distribution – consequences that are linked with fundamental issues of social policy, planning and the exercise of power and social control in the societies and the communities served by the educational systems under review. But above all the volume concludes, with some optimism, that an ecological perspective can help us to answer the elusive question: 'What difference does education make?'

Conclusion

This chapter has argued the case for an ecological study of education, suggesting that in our search for explanatory variables for differences in educational achievement we have failed to take adequate account of the distribution of educational resources and the nature of the response to these resources. The feasibility of such a study has been considered as have its potential difficulties and prospective contribution to understanding.

2

The ecological distribution of education

Can the distribution and response to educational resources offer an alternative source of explanation for differences in opportunity and achievement? Can the ecology of schooling lead to an enhanced understanding of the ecology of attainment? Is it possible to relate more fully the inputs of education to its ouputs? Douglas in *The Home and the School* (1964) noted that half of the 'inequalities' at eleven-plus appeared to spring from differences in secondary school provision. Certainly there is no lack of evidence of the existence of these differences or of their apparent consequences throughout education systems. A well-known example lies in the difference in the percentages of pupils entering higher education from the schools of different English and Welsh local education authorities. In 1960 the percentage ranged from 24·9 per cent in Cardiganshire to 5·1 per cent in the Isle of Ely for the counties, and from 17·9 per cent in Oxford to 1·7 per cent in West Ham for the county boroughs. In 1973–4, 15·3 per cent of all school leavers from the Northern region of England and 16·6 per cent from the Yorkshire and Humberside region entered full-time further education (universities, teacher training, colleges and other further education establishments). In the South East (excluding London) and the South West, the percentages were 23·7 and 24·6 respectively. A survey undertaken for the

Robbins Committee (1963) showed that such variations were not so much a reflection of differences in student ability between the areas, as has often been supposed, but a response to differences in local authority provision and practice. In particular they were significantly related to the number of grammar school places provided by the local authority. In areas where more than 23 per cent of the pupils went to grammar schools, 11 per cent of the whole age group entered higher education. In areas where grammar school entry was low – 18 per cent of the age group or under – only 7·5 per cent entered higher education. The differences remained even though social class variables were held constant.

Even within local authority areas there are differences. The Robbins Committee also reported that the West Riding of Yorkshire could be divided into three areas for selective purposes – areas of high, medium or low intake into the selective schools. The test requirements for entry into selective schools were highest where the selective entry was lowest. Yet a higher percentage went to higher education from the areas of high and medium intake, suggesting that an important variable is not only the ability of the students at age eleven but also the local availability of places in schools which prepare students to enter higher education.

The implications of the consequences of differential provision of educational resources were clearly seen in the major debates on education and opportunity in the 1960s. In Britain perhaps the most notable public recognition occurred through the concept of the *Educational Priority Areas* introduced in the Plowden Report (1967) which advocated a strategy of 'enriching areas where the availability and response to educational and other social resources seemed to be markedly below the norms for the community as a whole. Characteristically such areas were the old inner city zones of the large industrial conurbations. It was believed that the 'disadvantaged' children of such areas could be 'compensated' by the provision of schools with better equipment and facilities and more and better paid teachers.

The proposition that good schools should make up for a poor environment is far from new. It derives from the notion that there should be equality of opportunity for all, but recognizes that children in some districts will only get the same opportunity as those who live elsewhere if they have unequally generous treatment. It was accepted before the First World War that some children could not be effectively taught until they had been properly fed. Hence free meals were provided. Today their need is for enriched intellectual nourishment. Planned and positive discrimination in favour of deprived areas could bring about an advance in the education of children in the 1970s as great as the advance in their nutrition to which school meals and milk contributed so much. (Plowden Report, 1967)

Yet the case, though impressively argued, was by no means fully substantiated in detail and despite the early emergence of several charismatic leaders in the various priority areas and considerable local enthusiasm the results of intervention, though occasionally impressive, were generally inconclusive. Accompanied by widespread disillusion with Headstart and other similar intervention strategies in North American systems the outcomes led to a considerable diminution of interest and a realization that the Plowden analysis was not only too simple but also unclear in its understanding of political and social realities. It is only in the more coherent and grounded interpretations of interaction strategies available since the publications of the detailed findings of the Education Priority Project (Halsey, 1972) that a more realistic consideration of 'ecological' or 'resource' engineering may be undertaken.

The development of ecological consciousness

An essential starting point for a proper consideration of such strategies is a clear map of the nature of the ecological distribution of resources. Despite such visible clues to the significance of resource variation, the attempts to produce such a map have been incomplete. An important task of this chapter is to review and draw together the sporadic explorations that exist.

There has been documentation of unevenness in educational provision for a considerable period of time. The Argyll Commission Report (1869), which presaged the 1872 act setting up a national system of education in Scotland, recorded widespread differences in educational provision throughout Scotland over a century ago. The Report was able to document a wide range of variables that arose not only from the distribution of both national and local public funds but also from denominational, demographic and economic factors. The Report drew particular attention to the way in which these factors combined to produce markedly different situations in the Highlands at one end of the scale and in Glasgow at the other. In England and Wales the political events that led up to the passage of the 1870 act that introduced universal compulsory education were informed by a similar awareness of the widespread unevenness not only in education but in the very opportunity for education of any kind.

Much of the history of education for the past century has focused on the debate on the continuance of unevenness in resource distribution – a debate in which typically the participants are divided into those who seek to justify unevennesses and those who advocate their alleviation and seek a means of implementing it. Boyle (1967) has reviewed some of the national strategies that have ensued including the tax equalization and block grant arrangements that have been introduced by various governments. At local government level local redistribution strategies such as the closure of small rural schools and the successive reorganization of elementary and secondary schools have become a familiar feature of local politics. Coupled with the gradual process of legislation to enforce compulsory attendance, to raise the school leaving age and to introduce more uniform arrangements for schooling such as 'secondary education for all', and augmented by developments in professionalism such as longer teacher training and the elimination of uncertified teachers, there has been an evident attempt to move towards a more even distribution of resources. Yet differences persisted, as the well-known political arithmetic volumes of Gray and Moshinsky of the 1930s (1938) and the social mobility studies of Glass in the late 1940s and early 1950s (1954) demonstrate clearly. In the 1960s, Peaker (1967) and Wiseman (1964) made pioneering efforts to identify environmental factors of children and relate them to their attainment in school. Such studies were, matching the ethic of the period, 'child-centred' and presented a more fragmented picture of the distribution of resources than that displayed by subsequent studies.

The ecological map makers

Of greater assistance at this point in the volume are the detailed surveys of Taylor and Ayres (1969) and Pratt, Burgess, Allemano and Locke (1973) which have shown the widespread regional and

26

local variations in educational expenditure, class size, further education provision, pre-school education and much else. A particularly valuable source for surveys of educational provision are the local authority statistics issued annually by the Chartered Institute of Public Finance and Accountancy (formerly the Institute of Municipal Treasurers and Accountants) which provide a remarkably clear picture of the spending patterns and financial resources of local education authorities in England and Wales. The figures of the Institute along with the detailed annual *Statistics of Education* published by the Department of Education and Science have facilitated many important studies, including the forward planning exercises instituted by the Local Government Operational Research Unit (Myers, 1969) and the development of a number of planning models for education which are usefully reviewed by Armitage and Williams (1976).

The work of Taylor and Ayres (1969) provides perhaps the most useful starting point. Reviewing the English and Welsh statistics for the late 1960s, the authors bring together a comprehensive picture of the differences in the material and social environment that appeared likely to affect the educational opportunities of children. They identified six main factors that were susceptible to investigation:

1. The level of health, physical and mental, enjoyed by parents and children.
2. The standard of social services; included among these are housing, medical and welfare services.
3. The standard of local prosperity measured in terms of (a) personal incomes, and (b) income available to the local authority.
4. Local opportunities for, and variety of, employment both for school leavers and adults.
5. Population dynamics, i.e. increase or decrease in population, migration, density of population, social class structure and fertility.
6. The prevailing level of literacy among parents, relatives, employers and local leaders.

Against these factors the quality of educational provision was assessed. Taylor and Ayres comment: 'Standards far below the average, whether physical, social or economic, affect the quality of education both demanded and provided. They determine alike the attitude of parents and children towards education and the

27

willingness of elected representatives to spend money on education.'

A wide range of national and local statistical sources were assembled to provide evidence of the distribution of the factors and, using them, the authors present in careful detail a picture of regional differences in which the variations in one factor are almost reinforced by the others. Not only does their book present an insight into the interlocking and cumulative nature of ecological differences; it also provides many practical examples of the difficulty of alleviating them. Thus, in the discussion of public library services, Taylor and Ayres point out:

> The enthusiasm of generous authorities can be better appreciated when it is realized that Burnley and Oldham, Hull and Lincoln, Liverpool and Halifax devote a sixpenny rate to libraries while Reading and Oxford are able to provide a service of similar standard at the cost of a threepenny rate ...; it is not unfair to conclude that whether a child has access in a public library to the books he needs is a matter of chance, depending on where he lives.

This reference to the differences in 'situation' between local education authorities alerts us to the extreme caution with which comparisons must be made. Expenditure on resources can only be considered meaningfully in relation to the assets and needs of the authority at the start of the period under review. Does the area already have a good stock of well equipped, recently built schools with modern facilities? Does it have a growing, static or declining child population? Unless such questions are taken into account then an area with massive spending may still be providing its children with educational resources below the national average whilst a parsimonious authority may still offer its children a favoured environment.

The work of Taylor and Ayres showed a clear relationship between the general ecological environment and the specific environment of the schools. Thus, the North West borough of Burnley was seen to need the replacement of one house in two. The evidence of the material conditions of the schools suggested that a similar proportion of primary school places needed replacement. Conversely, areas with a favourable housing stock were, in general, characterized by a favourable school material environment (a pattern of distribution that had earlier been noted by the Newsom Committee (1963) in its examination of secondary schools). Much the same picture is painted for teacher supply (though the tendency of some of the less favoured North region boroughs to 'grow their own teachers' alleviates their situation), the existence of independent schools, university and polytechnic provision and even places for handicapped children.

The consequences of such differential position, though properly the subject of the next chapter of this book, are already clearly to be seen in the Taylor and Ayres analysis – in particular, the incidence of staying on after minimum school leaving age and of entry to post school education. But it is an important feature of their analysis that this differential response in itself may constitute a contributory factor for the general ecological problems of the environment – both social and economic as well as specifically educational ones.

Regional variations

Bringing these findings together in the framework of the standard regions of England and Wales, Taylor and Ayres write of the North and North West regions:

> In the Northern region, earnings and personal incomes are low, families tend to be large and unemployment is above average. Since rateable value is low, income available to local authorities is below average despite rate support grant designed to even out local authority income. Opportunities for earning a high income are limited and variety of employment for school leavers is similarly limited. Migration from the region has continued over a long period; the exodus has included the more able, ambitious and highly skilled. In the Tyneside conurbation in particular, health is below average, housing standards are low, school buildings far from modern.
>
> The majority of children leave school early. The region produces a large number of teachers (many of whom migrate on completion of training) though only a small number of graduates. The combined effect of migration, environmental deficiencies and lack of educational opportunities has resulted in a generation of parents whose level of education is low. Their understanding of the need for change and of the long term advantages of education is inevitably limited.
>
> The major environmental problem of the North Western region, second only to that of the low level of personal and

public income, is housing. All three contribute to a high rate of ill health and mortality; in spite of massive migration, unemployment has been persistent over a long period; families are large; supporting health services are insufficient. Because a large proportion of schools date back to the last century, the need for replacement schools is greater here than anywhere else in the country. The number of children remaining at school for extended courses is larger than in the Northern region but not noticeably so. Like the Northern region, the North West is a major producer of teachers though it takes up less than its due share of university places. Social, educational and environmental inequalities between one area and another within the region are marked. The outstanding feature of the region is the concentration of every conceivable unfavourable environmental factor in the two large conurbations. Although they produce disastrous effects on education, the problems are not primarily educational nor can they be solved by educational reform....

The Southern regions, comprising just under half the country's population, evince a positive attitude to education deriving, probably, more from a realization of the material advantages it brings than from an appreciation of the social benefits of an educated community. In most parts of the three regions educational and environmental conditions are favourable: well educated and prosperous parents; new schools adequately staffed and equipped; variety of employment; few legacies of the industrial revolution. Consequently the majority of children are able to realize their potentialities, although it is possible that the less able child is no better catered for than elsewhere – in view of the generally higher standards of achievement he may, in fact, be more conscious of failure.

Though the Taylor and Ayres figures are already some six to eight years old at the time of writing and many striking changes have occurred in the socio-economic condition of England and Wales, not least in the distribution of unemployment and other crucial factors, there is little evidence to suggest that there has been any fundamental relative change in the distributive map they have drawn.

educational resource – access to entry to public examinations. His study showed widespread variations in the opportunity of children in different schools and in different local education authorities to compete in these important determinants of life chance. Some local authorities severely restricted exam entries in their non-selective schools; one authority expressly restricted entry to public examinations to its grammar schools and further education colleges, pupils wishing to take such examinations having to transfer, usually after minimum leaving age. Other authorities encouraged all schools to develop examination courses, offering more generous staffing ratios and capitation grants to facilitate them. Some schools adopted policies of entry 'only for those with a good chance of success'; others entered all who wanted 'to have a go'. In consequence, chances of examination success seemed to depend at least as much on ecological environment as on ability. The research showed clearly that the incidence of examination success as a proportion of the total age cohort was strikingly greater in those areas and in those schools where open entry policies prevail – a finding that is reinforced by the subsequence experience of comprehensive schooling (Neave, 1975).

Resource allocation within the local education authority

It is not only between local education authorities that differences occur; there are also differences within them. Until recently the secondary education of most authorities was divided between modern schools and grammar schools; in almost every case the per capita resource allocation to the grammar school was ahead of that of the modern school. The extent of the differentiation was almost wholly a matter of local education policy and depended on which of the many possible interpretations of the concept of 'parity of esteem' was adopted. And even though this differentiation will disappear as comprehensivization spreads, many other differences remain. Most primary schools receive a substantially lower per capita rate than most secondary schools; allowances are generally higher for old pupils and public examination candidates. Higher rates for boys than girls have almost wholly disappeared but only recently. The ratio of building size to school numbers also varies in similar ways to the capitation allowances as do the special allowances for teachers' salaries and the ratios of ancillary staff. In addition to the local policy differences on these issues from area to area there may well be historical and social

A parent's perspective

A parallel study to that of Taylor and Ayres is that of Pratt, Burgess, Allemano and Locke (1973). They offer a parent's guide to differences in educational provision – an important service to a geographically mobile society. Taking the English local authorities of Doncaster, Bootle and Wiltshire they illustrate the quite different provisions that parents may expect to find for their children in these areas. They demonstrate that these differences – in school, teachers, systems of organization and much else – arise not only from the general ecological variations between the authorities but also from the specific variations that arise from within the educational services – traditions, methods of interpretation, enthusiasm for some permitted but not mandatory provisions but not others. In short, there comes to be an 'administrative climate' of the various areas which becomes a crucial factor in determining the educational ecology of the area. Byrne, Williamson and Fletcher (1975) adopt yet a further related perspective. In *The Poverty of Education* they explore the theme that the differential attainments of children from different social class backgrounds are largely explained by real differences in the kinds and quality of educational resources made available to them. This leads them to a study of the distribution of education that has close parallels with the work of Taylor and Ayres and of Pratt, Burgess, Allemano and Locke. Though using many of the measures adopted by these writers and others closely related to them, they go somewhat further in the identification of administrative climate suggesting that this may override and often distort the more direct and measurable economic variables that distinguish local authorities:

Whether by conscious policy or the contingencies of replacing physical capital, projects emerge within a local authority which attract resources and prestige, and which inevitably detract from many other facets of an LEA.... It is only possible to detect the thread of policy which underlies such projects, be they sixth form colleges or community schools. However, intensive local studies are required, which attempt to uncover the constraints operating upon the development of policy and the process of decision making itself.

A typology of local education authorities

Taking educational provisions, policy, attainment and class background into account, Byrne, Williamson and Fletcher suggest six 'clusters' of local authorities. Of these the first two contrasting clusters will suffice to indicate the nature of the typology they offer:

Cluster 1

The areas falling into cluster 1 are unequivocally working class, and predominantly Labour controlled. These are the towns so often described as the depressed industrial areas of Britain, the industrialization and depression seemingly inseparable. . . .

The poor material environment of these areas is evidenced by high population and household densities and the poverty of social amenities in the community.

LEAs in such areas, although varying to some degree in the type and quality of their educational provision, sustain this picture of relative deprivation. The attainment rates for such areas are characteristically low, both in terms of the numbers of children remaining at school beyond the statutory minimum leaving age, and in terms of numbers entering further and higher education. Where the level of unemployment is high, teenage unemployment or increasing mobility is likely to be a common feature of these areas. . . .

Expenditure tends to be concentrated upon secondary education with consequently low provision for primary education. However, pupil/teacher ratios for both primary and secondary schools are average.

LEAs falling into this cluster would include *Barnsley, Bootle, Merthyr Tydfil, Norwich, South Shields and Wigan*.

Cluster 2

The social class background of areas in cluster 2 is clearly non-manual, and largely upper middle class. Such areas are likely to have a highly mobile population. Significantly, LEAs falling into this cluster are counties, rather than county boroughs, largely concentrated in the south. These areas embrace the rich suburbs and commuter belts serving large industrial centres. They are typically Conservative controlled authorities, with a minimal degree of industrialization. Housing is predictably largely owner-occupied, and the high rateable value of such areas reflects the high quality of soci amenities. . . .

The types of school complement the wealth of the area, wi a high proportion of direct grant and independent schools.

The quality of educational provision in terms of per pu expenditure is high, although expenditure on teachers' sala is below the national average, which probably reflects available supply of teachers in such areas.

Rates of attainment conform to these high standards in te of high rates of staying on beyond sixteen and seventeen of age. Entry to further and higher education similarly re high achievement, particularly entrance to university.

Though offered tentatively and with many reservations th little doubt that the clusters offer a vignette of some characteristics of different types of local authority.

Staying on at school

Eggleston (1974a) conducted an exploration of the e factors likely to be associated with staying on in English ary schools. In this study the focus was not so much on th or on the local education authorities but on the catchm of specific schools in a large area of the North and East Two main clusters of factors were explored. One was economic status of the school catchment area (measure Index – at the time of the survey a particularly useful ir eligibility for juror service depending upon occupati perty above a threshold rateable value proved a soun of socio-economic status). The other cluster of fac characteristics of the local education administration the availability of places in comprehensive and selec the arrangements which existed for transfer between equipment and facilities of schools, and the pos courses offered.

The study will be reported in greater detail in Ch volume but it is relevant here to notice that, at t school level, the correlation between general back catchment area and the specific characteristics noted by the other writers already referred to in th strongly confirmed. But of particular interest v identification of unevenness in the distributio

reasons why the differences between schools are even greater, adding yet a further dimension of unevenness to an already fragmented ecological landscape.

Effective access to resources

A further exploration of ecological differences is that of Robinson (1976) who offers evidence to confirm the marked difference in effective availability of educational resources between those children who are labelled 'poor' and those who are not. Robinson adds yet an extra dimension to the discussion in his consideration not only of the effectiveness of supply but also of the effectiveness of demand. It is not enough for resources to be available, there has to be some means whereby they can be 'demanded' before an effective response to them takes place. The educational environment of the child who cannot take advantage of the educational resources in the intake class, whether it be the sophistication of the learning toys or the joys of the sand and water table, because his culture denies him either the knowledge or the confidence to use them, lives within at least as deprived an educational ecology as the child who has no access to these things. The mother who through ignorance or fear is unable to establish contact with the teacher to understand the strategies whereby her child is being offered an equal or even a favoured share of educational resources in the school or the community is likely to be restricted to a disadvantaged ecological environment regardless of the policies or spending patterns of local education authorities.

The Educational Priority Project

One of the most sharply focused reviews of differential educational provision was undertaken in conjunction with the Educational Priority Project which sprang from the conclusions of the Plowden Report. This major inquiry was funded by the Department of Education and Science and the Social Science Research Council and was conducted by Halsey (1972). In the study of the four Educational Priority Areas, it became clear that some of the most striking differences in social and educational provision were being identified. The published report presents a detailed account of overcrowded families lacking the exclusive use of basic amenities such as fixed baths, hot water taps and WCs, low family incomes (in Deptford and Birmingham), substantial numbers of recent immigrants and (in all but the West Riding area) a high pupil turnover and high absenteeism from schools. But one of the most notable findings was the distribution of child attainment which had been established even before the beginning of primary school life constituting an important feature of the ecological map of all four EPAs:

> Our own programme of testing in primary schools ... revealed that EPA five-year-olds were scoring well below national norms on a vocabulary test. This fact was brought home even more sharply when the scores on the same vocabulary test of children in pre-school groups in Birmingham EPA were compared with the scores of children in a playgroup in a middle class district. Even when immigrant children with language difficulties were excluded the mean standardized score of the EPA children was 93 points – seven points below the national mean – while the middle class children recorded a mean score of 108. On this basis the EPA children could be considered to be about a year behind the middle class children.

Another finding of particular interest arose from the exploration of the characteristics of teacher supply and their close relationships with the social ecology of the area. Thus the age distribution of teachers in the Educational Priority Areas primary schools contrasted with that for all primary schools in England and Wales. In the Deptford project schools 32 per cent of all teachers were under twenty-five, in Birmingham 27 per cent were under twenty-five, against the national average of 18 per cent of teachers in that age category. In Deptford 53 per cent of all teachers were under thirty-five and in Birmingham 67 per cent, as against the national average of 40 per cent. Associated with these figures there was a markedly high turnover of staff in the EPA primary schools. In Deptford 42 per cent stayed less than two years and in Birmingham 36 per cent stayed less than two years. In the two areas only 24 per cent and 25 per cent respectively stayed longer than five years. Teachers' perceptions of their jobs were also at variance with those not in Priority Areas:

> When comparing their jobs with those of friends, more teachers thought they were better off than thought they were worse off in respect of security, intellectual stimulation, opportunities to improve qualifications, and general satisfaction. Among these

aspects security gave the most satisfaction. More teachers thought they were worse off than thought they were better off in regard to social prestige, social stimulation, the neighbourhood in which they worked, physical conditions, pressure of work, present salary, salary scale as a whole, position as a whole including salary, and position as a whole excluding salary. The neighbourhood was the cause of the most dissatisfaction, but salary levels were also a major focus for discontent. Although the teachers tended to regard themselves as better off in regard to volume and hours of work, most of them thought that the pressure of work while they were actually on the job was worse than in other occupations. What is more remarkable, however, is the fact that nearly 60 per cent of respondents felt that their jobs yielded more general satisfaction than did the jobs which their friends held. This contrasts with only 16 per cent who thought that they were better off in terms of their position as a whole including salary. It seems that for EPA teachers psychological rewards are some compensation for low financial ones and poor working conditions.

Statistical hazards

Such conclusions offer a salutary reminder of the complex interrelationships that link ecology and behaviour and the dangers of oversimplified unidimensional pictures of inadequacy or disadvantage that may be drawn from the generation of statistical aggregates in the attempt to demonstrate the link between the distribution of educational resources and patterns of attainment or even class characteristics. To draw such a picture is not only to distort reality but also to ensure that the self-fulfilling image of 'being disadvantaged' becomes more widespread in the areas under consideration. Whilst a typology of local authorities may be a suggestive starting point for analyses it cannot indicate with sufficient precision the details of the actual resources that reach the individual school and the individual child and the effectiveness with which they are used. As Halsey concludes in his discussion of the EPA areas:

> They certainly suffer from multiple economic and social deprivations and their schools labour under difficulties brought into them by the characteristics of the surrounding neighbourhood. But there is no unique description of either the EPA or the

EPA school. . . . We therefore infer that the definition of the EPA, the diagnosis of its ills and the prescriptions for its amelioration must always be based on detailed local study.

Hutchinson (1975) in his critique of Byrne and Williamson's early work (1972) has drawn particular attention to the fallacy of statistical aggregates, writing:

> Firstly, there is one general point concerning the data which Byrne and Williamson use in all their papers. All the data are aggregated to LEA-level. The correlations they calculate are thus aggregate or ecological correlations. It is well known that these do not necessarily accord with individual correlations and in general have a tendency to exaggerate the magnitude of the effect compared with the latter. Moreover, some of the variables may properly be considered ecological, that is affecting the entire area (for example party in power) but others are merely aggregated. Taking an oversimplified example, to show that low social class acted on educational attainment through poverty of ecological resources rather than by socio-cultural effects, one would have to show that children of high social class parents also did badly in an area of low social class; one would have to examine the social class composition of those staying on until 16 to show that the differences could not be explained purely by the differences in social class proportions of the original cohort from which the 'stayers on' came.
>
> Thus, when Byrne and Williamson take high proportions of pupils staying on at school in an area of high social class and thus high educational provision as indicating that the provision is 'a major determinant' of educational attainment, they are committing classic examples of an 'ecological fallacy' since they cannot know from aggregate data who (or which social class) is staying on.

Though Byrne and Williamson defend themselves by claiming that they are concerned with cohorts not individuals, Hutchison's reminder of a well-known statistical trap is timely at this point where we have begun to see, with the aid of writers such as Halsey and Robinson, some of the shortcomings of the statistical surveys with which we began this chapter. Undoubtedly, if we are to reach a perceptive and usable understanding of the ecological distribution of education we must proceed beyond the aggregated survey data with which we began. Though an essential and even inescapable prelude to our considerations, such surveys are insufficient to provide a sensitive guide to the complex realities of human behaviour that spring from and ultimately create the ecological map of education. The way forward lies through consideration of the ways in which individuals, administrators, teachers, pupils and parents perceive their ecological environment and how in the light of their perceptions they respond to it and use it.

Individual perceptions

Such a view allows us to see that the concept of resources goes further than any list of quantifiable inputs, however extensive. It goes on to consider the ways in which resources are seen to have varying utility and meaning through the different *regimes* of local authorities. A comprehensive sixth form college in one system can be highly selective in admission policy; a similarly named establishment in another can have an 'open door' policy. The role of advisers in one authority can be strikingly different from that of another.

The significance of such a consideration of the different 'constructions' of apparently identical educational provision that parents and children occupying different standpoints in the social structure may hold, can be seen in an extract from the work of Jackson and Marsden on 'Marburton' School (1962):

As the eleven-plus drew nearer, one or two children were hurriedly moved across a vital boundary line, onto the side where there was more substantial grammar school provision. These were cases where the family had middle class relatives or friends. 'I never thought anything about this exam', said Mrs Waite, 'until Mrs Beardsell came down to talk to me. She was Peter Beardsell's mam, and he was our boy's age. She came down and she talked and she talked until in the end we took him away from that school and sent him to Broadbank.' But few parents were aware of these important discrepancies, and though many were looking forward hopefully to their child's success, others did not properly understand the significance of the exam.

Later in their book, Jackson and Marsden return again to the parents' perceptions of the education system and the consequences

Such parents were not wanting to know whether Anne could beat another girl in history, or whether she grasped the second law of thermodynamics. This information was welcome, and often useful – but it hung over a void. They wanted to know what physics *was*, and what kinds of jobs it opened for a girl; they wanted to know whether you could do anything with a history qualification except teach more history. They wanted to know the difference between a training college and a university, in nature, quality, time, cost. They wanted to know if their son could ever think of becoming a doctor after taking languages in the sixth form. Or what it meant in terms of future choice when their daughter had to abandon chemistry or Latin at thirteen; or whether there was any difference between the universities at Bangor and Oxford; or any difference between going into the civil service at eighteen or taking a degree first. A hundred and one problems of this kind troubled their relationship with school and child. We saw how often they misfired with teachers, how they were never likely to belong to the prevailing Parent/Teacher Association, how they turned in anxiety to relatives, neighbours, workmates, the clerk in the education offices.

It is clear that the 'Marburton' school system was in fact several fundamentally different systems to the population it served. The study of the ecology of schooling has a real need of a phenomenological perspective in that we are unavoidably concerned with important variations in the 'social construction of reality'. The reality of educational provision can be experienced in many different ways; the response to provision depends in part on the nature of these constructions. The distribution of educational resources is not just a product of the producer, but also, in an even more important sense, it is a product of the consumer.

Another early initiative which illuminates the dynamic relationship between consumer and producer of educational provision was Rogoff's *community context thesis* (1961):

It follows that each of the social classes will be more heavily concentrated in some kinds of community environments than in others, and that communities will vary in the predominant or average social class affiliation of their residents. Such structural differences may set in motion both formal arrangements

– such as school, library and general cultural facilities in the community – and informal mechanisms, such as normative climates or model levels of social aspiration, which are likely to affect *all* members of the community to some extent – parents and children, upper, middle and working class.

Social control and educational systems

At this point where we have introduced the interpretative as well as the positivist perspectives to ecological study, we can see more clearly the potential contribution that both can make to the sociological examination of educational systems. In doing so we can see in particular the issue of *social control* that underlies much of the subsequent argument of this volume. In the discussion of educational resources we are looking at nothing less than the process of the management, distribution and evaluation of knowledge. Educational systems are central instruments of social control in that they have, through the school system, a major role in making available or restricting the understandings, identities and opportunities that lead to the availability and exercise of power in modern societies. The detailed and complex ways in which control is exercised will be discussed in detail later in this volume. The discussion will include consideration of the distribution of examination facilities and course provision which throughout almost all school systems provide classic social control devices. All systems restrict, manifestly or latently, opportunities for accreditation or qualification, as Bowles and Gintis (1977) have observed. Along with the characteristic restrictions of examination syllabuses the consequences for the life chances of both the students who take the examination and those who do not are considerable. All systems offer different courses to different children, but the opportunities for the exercise of power and decision making between those who study programmes in language, literature and science and those who study programmes in the crafts, home economics and horticulture are likely to be strikingly different.

Viewed in this way the ecological map of education opens up new perspectives, not only on the nature and distribution of educational resources, and the ways in which they are perceived, but also on the distribution and exercise of power. It offers the prospect of an escape, on the one hand from the limited visions of the positivistic orientations and, on the other from the limited applicabilities of the non-positivistic approaches. Above all by demonstrating both the constructed nature of educational systems and reaffirming the importance of the structures, it reopens the consideration of change through education. It is an analysis that will be taken further in our consideration in subsequent chapters where we shall consider the responses to the ecology of distribution and the practices and policies which implement both distribution and response.

Conclusion

This chapter has considered the evidence of the ecological distribution of education and its relation to the more general socio-ecological environment in which education takes place. After reviewing the survey evidence available and the important contribution it offers, some of the problems of such data were explored and the development of more perceptive analyses of supply and demand of educational resources were considered.

3

The response to the ecological distribution

The distribution of the response to education is as uneven as the distribution of educational resources we studied in the previous chapter. Yet there are many indications of a relationship between the two distributions that suggest that there must be close links between them. The nature of these links is open to considerable debate. Some writers such as Byrne, Williamson and Fletcher see the link as unambiguously causal, claiming that the different rates of educational achievement of children from different social backgrounds are to a large extent explained by differences in the kind and equality of educational resources made available to them. Other writers such as Halsey see the linkage as potentially if not actually causal, whilst others such as Jencks see both resources and response as dependent variables – linked consequences of more fundamental causal factors in the social system. It will be easier to review these arguments at a later stage when we have considered in fuller detail the ecology of response which in any case is of such notable interest as to justify an early exploration in its own right.

The studies referred to in the previous chapter were all concerned to examine response as well as distribution and it will be useful to turn to them again to seek illumination for this chapter. Taylor and Ayres tell us of the striking variations between examination results in the various regions. They note that in the Northern region of England barely 10 per cent of the boys and only just over 5 per cent of girls obtained the traditional passport to higher education – two or more A levels – and that only 16 per cent of all school leavers went on to some form of full-time continuing education. Conversely, in the South East region (excluding London) the figures show that 15 per cent of boys and 10 per cent of girls obtained two or more A level passes and over 22 per cent of all school leavers continued some form of full-time education.

The regional differences in examination successes have persisted in the period since the Taylor and Ayres survey. In 1973–4 the percentages of school leavers going to employment with neither GCE passes nor CSE achievements of Grade 5 or better were as follows:

Wales	31·2
Yorkshire and Humberside	23·5
West Midlands	23·4
London	19·5
South West	17·0
South East (excluding London)	15·3

Distribution of university awards also shows a pronounced regional variation, though this was alleviated to some extent by somewhat greater preference for teacher training college entry in the Northern regions. The regional variation in entry to the universities of Oxford and Cambridge is particularly marked, coming predominantly from the South East region including London – a figure reflecting not only the unevennesses in the distribution of state education but also the uneven distribution of private education – the public schools having particularly close links with colleges at Oxford and Cambridge. The notable differences between the Northern and Southern regions of England and Wales are to be seen in many other areas, particularly in the differential expenditure of local authorities on assistance to students at universities and similar institutions.

Variations in 'staying on' at school

But one of the most striking variations in the distribution of educational response, which is noted not only by Taylor and Ayres, but also by Pratt, Burgess, Allemano and Locke and most other investigators, concerns the crucial variable of 'staying on' at secondary school after minimum leaving age. All investigators are unanimous on the strikingly uneven distribution of response that the figures of various local authorities and schools reveals. The significance of this variable is widely recognized. Weinberg (1969) in the British Sociological Association study *Comparability and Social Research* concluded 'the most significant educational variable is one which combines terminal educational age with "staying on".' Throughout the 1950s and 1960s the rise in voluntary staying on at school after minimum leaving age was striking. Such epithets as 'the explosion in demand' or 'the voluntary raising of the school leaving age' were used to describe the trend. Though the rise in staying on was great in almost all areas of England and Wales, the markedly great rise in some areas such as the South East had the net effect of increasing rather than reducing the disproportionate educational opportunities available to children in different parts of the country.

Initially the differences were often a consequence of the different educational policies of the local education authorities – some actively seeking to encourage continued staying on at school by provision of extended courses of wide variety and others striving to contain and even minimize demand. Yet after the initial waves the response itself came to be the major factor in many areas, obliging local authorities to devote additional resources in order to satisfy it. Not only did the trend change the ecological map of demand but also the ecological map of supply of resources.

In the 1970s the situation is less noticeable. The rise in voluntary staying on was inevitably muted by the compulsory raising of the school leaving age in 1971 and has undoubtedly been reduced still further by the worsening economic conditions in the mid 1970s, especially those for qualified personnel. But quite apart from these, the simple statistical characteristic of demand 'levelling out' as it approaches unity levels has also been in evidence.

Yet the widespread differences which first attracted the attention of observers in the 1950s and 1960s still remain and constitute one of the notable areas of differential response to education. Inevitably the pattern of differences is complex. Though simply and usefully expressed in terms of regional variations, in fact variations within regions are often more striking than those between them. Much depends upon local education authority policy. In general, high staying on is predictably concentrated in grammar schools and is less in secondary modern schools. But an interesting result emerged from the research of Eggleston (1974a). In this study it had been assumed that a high provision of grammar school places allowing guaranteed opportunity to stay on for extended courses would effectively drain off the local demand for extended education; in consequence the instance of extended courses at the non-selective secondary modern schools in those areas would tend to be small. In fact this was not the case. In such areas a high rate of entry to selective schools was associated with a high demand for and a high rate of staying on in the non-selective secondary modern schools. This evidence suggested that the effective demand for extended education was not tied to a limited supply of pupils 'who can benefit from it' but rather seemed to be a demand which grew in response to the existence of educational opportunity. Much the same consequence was noted in the areas in which comprehensive schooling with built in opportunity for entry to extended courses for all pupils was introduced. Here the rate of staying on was generally higher than in any area where the division of secondary schools into grammar and modern existed. Neave in his more recent study of comprehensive schools and extended courses has confirmed this finding (1975), drawing attention to the very wide range of extended courses for which students stay on in comprehensive schools.

The significance of the distribution of staying on is of course far greater than the differences in immediate educational opportunities that arise. A wide variety of studies on school leavers repeatedly confirm the differences in life chance that spring from extended schooling. Barber (1968), in a study of school leavers in Oxford, showed clearly the divergent paths followed by those who left school early at minimum leaving age and those who stayed on.

Staying on and resource provision

Whilst Taylor and Ayres, like Pratt, Burgess, Allemano and Locke and many other writers, seek to demonstrate that the total material environment and the specific educational environment of children play a major part in determining or enhancing their educational life chance through differences in staying on, entry to higher education and other variables, a number of writers have attempted to explore the relationship more precisely. Eggleston

(1974a) and Byrne, Williamson and Fletcher (1975) have sought to explore precise indicators of local, environmental and administrative factors and correlate them with specific measures of attainment – Eggleston at school level and Byrne, Williamson and Fletcher at the local authority level. Eggleston explored three response variables:

- (a) Extent of staying on after minimum leaving age, expressed as a percentage of the total age cohort in the school in the previous year.
- (b) Extent of staying on a second year, expressed as a percentage of the total age cohort in the school two years previously.
- (c) Change in the rate of staying on in the school during the survey period.

He related these to ten school administrative and socio-economic variables:

1 Sex of pupils.
2 Size of school.
3 Intake of pupils to selective schools from the non-selective school catchment areas.
4 The extent of staying on after sixteen in selective schools drawing pupils from the non-selective catchment areas.
5 Material environment of the schools. This was a ranking of the specialist teaching facilities available in each school undertaken on similar lines to the survey reported in the *Newsom Report* (1963). In each case the ranking was undertaken by two independent assessors, the few differences being resolved by investigation of the school by the writer.
6 Age of school building. Again following Newsom precedent, schools were asked to report the approximate date of the construction of the earliest part of the school buildings in current use.
7 Provision of extended courses.
8 Success rates in GCE examinations taken in the fifth year of extended courses.
9 Success rates in non GCE examinations.
10 Socio-economic status of the catchment area. This was established by applying the Juror Index to the total population of the catchment area of each school.

47

Byrne, Williamson and Fletcher identified three measures of educational attainment: the proportion of pupils remaining at school beyond sixteen years, the proportion of pupils remaining at school beyond seventeen years, and 'rates of entry' into different forms of higher education.

They linked them with eight local environmental variables:

1 Degree of industrialization.
2 Proportion of domestic hereditaments where rateable value is below £101.
3 Comparative size of rate deficiency grant.
4 Population size.
5 Population density.
6 Proportion of households inhabited at high density.
7 Proportion of shared dwellings with all basic amenities.
8 Proportion of all dwellings with all basic amenities.

Four local authority policy variables were also added:

1 The amount of rates called in in relation to the total rateable value of LEA areas.
2 The extent of Labour control of the authority.
3 The proportion of households in the area resident in council houses.
4 The proportion of children aged thirteen in comprehensive schools.

Both groups of investigators found close correlation between their variables.

Eggleston found that the correlations between the incidence of staying on and the administrative variables in the period prior to the raising of the school leaving age to sixteen were as set out in Table 3.1. Not surprisingly, the most highly significant correlations were those between staying on and the provision of identified extended courses; indeed this provision and the factors associated with it emerged as being of overriding importance in the incidence of staying on.

Also significant were the size, condition and age of the school buildings. Of the three, school size was most closely correlated with staying on, being significant at the 1 per cent level for all three indicators. Large schools were closely identified with high rates of staying on, particularly with staying on after sixteen. The underlying factors here seemed to be the advantages in running examination courses which large schools enjoy. These were

Table 3.1 *Administrative variables and staying on. Bilateral and secondary modern schools. Product moment correlation coefficients (r)*

Variable	Staying on one year	Staying on two years	Rate of change in staying on
School size ★	0·2846	0·3571	0·2175
Intake of selective ★ schools in same area	0·0511	0·0021	0·0297
Staying on after 16 in selective schools in same area ★	0·0720	0·0906	0·0783
School material environment ★	0·3086	0·1507	0·1829
Age of school buildings ★	0·2844	0·1244	0·1607
Extended course provision †	0·6525	0·6341	0·4180
GCE exam successes †	0·5375	0·5409	0·3859
Non GCE exam successes †	0·4495	0·2890	0·4495

★ Variables examined for 240 schools.
† Variables examined for 125 schools (all schools in Coventry, Derby, SE Derbyshire, Leicester, Leicestershire and Nottingham).

particularly relevant in the modern schools, where the generous staffing and facilities needed to launch an examination course successfully had to be 'spared' initially from elsewhere in the school. Only in a large school could this 'sparing' be done without obvious sacrifice of the non-examination majority. Moreover, the large school had advantages in attracting academically qualified staff by virtue of its higher allowance of special responsibility posts. The spiral of events, once established, continued. Academic staff could be offered academic work and the higher points total which the extended course pupils allowed could still further facilitate staff recruitment.

The school material environment – an index of the quality of specialist teaching facilities of the school – was also significantly correlated with all three indicators at the 15 per cent level. The age of the school buildings was also highly significant for all three indicators, the older the buildings the fewer pupils staying on and the lesser rate of increase. Both factors were, interestingly, far more highly significant for staying on after fifteen than for staying on after sixteen. The age and condition of the school buildings seemed to be more important factors in the initial decision to stay on than in subsequent decisions. At sixteen-plus the pupils seemed to have internalized the goals of the school and become relatively indifferent to the architecture.

Correlation or causality?

The existence of correlation between socio-economic and administrative factors and response was further explored by Byrne, Williamson and Fletcher using the clusters of local education authorities to which reference has already been made. They drew up correlation tables showing the relationships between their three 'response indicators' and the range of socio-economic and administrative variables for the local education authority areas under review. The correlation tables for the sixteen-plus cohort, the seventeen-plus cohort and the nineteen-plus cohort indicate, for the most part, relationships that would now have been anticipated by readers of this book. Commenting upon this Byrne, Williamson and Fletcher suggest:

the social-class background of an LEA influences the attainment of cohorts of school-children passing through its schools and in the following ways:

1 Directly, i.e. in terms of 'personal', socio-cultural and familiar inputs,
2 Through the relationship between social-class background and environmental factors,
3 Through the relationship between social-class background and educational provision,
4 Through the relationship between social-class background, educational policy and educational provision.

With the exception of the relationship of class with policy/provision/attainment, we would normally (in terms of our views on the nature of the educational socio-spatial system) think of high social class as being associated with good provision, good environmental conditions and high attainment. However, low social class could be associated with radical policy, high provision and good attainment.

Byrne, Williamson and Fletcher proceed, with the aid of a range of multi-variant procedures which are set out in detail in their book, to claim to have established a causal model as follows:

50

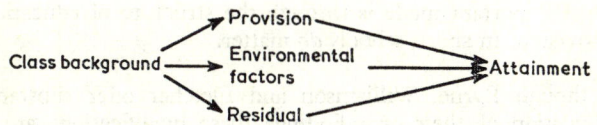

Class background, provision, environmental conditions and attainment

They add several notes of qualification to this model however. In particular, the size and unknown nature of the residual factor presents a difficulty – a difficulty that was also to be seen in Peaker's analysis of environmental factors for the Plowden Committee studies (Peaker, 1967). In Byrne, Williamson and Fletcher's study the residual is in some areas substantial; for example in its affect of the rate of staying on for boys at sixteen-plus. This leads them to an important commentary on their results:

> The character of the residual cannot be determined from our data. It clearly does include the social and cultural character-istics of groups of people, but it cannot refer entirely to such characteristics. The reason for this is obvious. As we have shown in Chapter 5 and subsequent chapters, the kind of policy a local authority pursues influences the extent and character of what it provides. This provision, in turn, is related to measures of educational attainment. Where provision is high there is a tendency for attainment to be high. Seen from this perspective, high levels of provision can be thought of as influencing the demand for education. Certainly, when provision and environ-mental measures are taken into account, the importance of class-background variables by themselves is reduced signifi-cantly.

In the light of these results the conclusions of Byrne, Williamson and Fletcher are somewhat more modest than those anticipated in their earlier chapters. They write:

> ... our results so far suggest that the level of educational pro-vision in local authority areas has a very direct bearing on educational life chances of children in those areas.

> ... When education and environment are equal, the influences of class background on the attainment of children in different LEA areas is markedly reduced. Such equality, of course, is rarely if ever found in practice. The argument therefore is about the mode of influence of class background upon edu-cational attainment. Our results lead to the suggestion that the

51

most important mode is through the structure of educational provision. In short, schools *do* matter.

Yet though Byrne, Williamson and Fletcher offer substantial qualification of their own findings these qualifications are insufficient to satisfy their many critics who find their demonstration of causality crude and unproven. We have already referred to Hutchison's (1975) critique of the earlier work of Byrne and Williamson. Pyle (1975) has also drawn attention to a range of other difficulties such as a failure to measure the distribution of resources between schools – difficulties which are not fully solved in the more recent work under review in this volume. Yet as a preliminary explanation of a complex area Byrne, Williamson and Fletcher's work stands as a useful prelude to more sophisticated overall analyses of ecological consequences.

The Leicestershire Plan – a case study

Certainly the likelihood that provision and environment are factors that both reflect and augment social class differences is one that is reaffirmed by many studies. In Eggleston's (1974a) account of the Leicestershire Plan the findings certainly offer such reaffirmation showing, as they do, a clear example of how social class variables are mediated by the nature of provision and environment.

Under the 'Leicestershire Plan' children wishing to follow a continuing education had to transfer from the comprehensive 'high' school providing education only to the statutory minimum leaving age to the comprehensive 'upper' school providing a range of courses leading to public examinations, higher education and professional careers. In any kind of neighbourhood, the children of non-manual workers tend to have the higher rate of transfer to the upper schools. But as a study of the Oadby and Wigston areas showed, the rate for manual workers' children is higher in a middle class neighbourhood than in a working class one. Conversely the rate for non-manual workers is lower in the working class area than the middle class area. The effect of environment as well as provision on the response of children from different social class backgrounds is unmistakable (see Table 3.2). In view of these figures, it is not surprising that the social composition of the single upper school to which all these children transferred is markedly different from that of the high schools. At the time of the survey, 44 per cent of the pupils in the upper school serving the three communities were middle class.

A further question arose. Were the middle and working class pupils who rejected continued education those who had been

Table 3.2 *Fathers' occupations related to children transferred to upper school*

%	Middle class community	Socially mixed community	Working class community
Fathers manual workers	59·1	38·3	30·0
Fathers non-manual workers	82·2	78·0	77·5

relegated to lower streams in the high school? Table 3.3 relates stream positions (A, B or C) to transfer decisions. More children transferred to upper schools from A streams. And the A streams were predominantly middle class, with C streams being chiefly working class. But here again the response was more than might have been expected. The proportion of C stream pupils choosing to extend their education would have been rare in the corresponding part of a non-comprehensive system (the lower half of a secondary modern school). The Leicestershire figure for C streams compared well with the 21 per cent of all secondary modern school pupils staying on after the minimum leaving age in the same period.

Table 3.3 *Stream positions related to transfer decisions*

	A %	B %	C %
Transferred	84	59·15	26.6
Not transferred	16	40·85	73·4

A still further question arose. Did these figures conceal a 'class waste of ability' occurring at the point of transfer over and above the 'waste' normally associated with streaming? Of the A streams, 95 per cent of the non-manual pupils transferred, but only 75 per cent of the manual workers' children. This apparent 'class waste of ability' is reminiscent of the premature leaving reported by the British grammar schools in the early 1950s. In many grammar schools the 'waste' has now been largely deferred or eliminated. Many comprehensive schools still have to achieve this holding power and are handicapped in doing so by the lack of early commitment to extended education that under earlier arrangements sprang from successes at the eleven-plus selection examination. This and the immediate attractions of leaving school at sixteen-plus may lead the student not to transfer. The values of the working class home and peer group may not always question his decision carefully. Conversely, the middle class child is rather more likely to be supported in transfer by home values and by the educational experience of his parents. Again the 'class chance' of the child seemed to be powerfully affected by provision and environment.

Explicit and implicit demand for resources

In considering Eggleston's research we have reached an understanding that a more sensitive ecological perspective is one that is conceived around demand rather than response alone, emphasizing the active rather than the passive role of the individual. E. M. Byrne (1976) has drawn attention to the two way link between demand and resources noting that not only does limitation of resources depress demand but also dynamic demand creates or attracts resources. She distinguishes two kinds of demand for resources. One is the *explicit* demand from individuals or groups who know what they want and make their views heard – demands for sports facilities, ballroom dancing classes and workshop facilities. The other *implicit* demand represents the needs, often incompletely diagnosed, of those who are unable or unwilling to ask for them – or of those who may be unaware of the potential advantage of using educational resources. These may include the illiterate, the innumerate, the immigrants and many other partially 'submerged' categories. But other implicit demands may commonly arise from incompletely provided resources in most other areas of educational provision. Why, for example, do the local education authority evening classes in a middle class suburb provide a far wider range of courses than those in many working class districts?

Size and response

Just as it is important to emphasize demand as well as response, so too it is important not to focus the whole discussion of ecology

54

on the consideration of social class. Quite apart from the obvious difficulties in achieving a commonly acceptable definition of social class (which give Byrne, Williamson and Fletcher, like most other investigators, many problems) it also leads to a myopia that may fail to see the many other consequences of differential provision of education that may be largely unconnected with class. David (1976) draws attention to one of these: the relationship between the size of the unit of provision – class, school or administrative area – and the effective response associated with it. She writes:

Since the origins of state provision of education in 1870 in Britain there has been a continuous political dispute about the appropriate size of local community necessary to support effective schools and supply resources efficiently to them. But throughout the history of the debate the size question has never been resolved because it has been used by politicians to support different values about the nature of local as opposed to central government control of the education system. Moreover, participants, e.g. teachers as a professional body, other than elective representatives have also contributed to the size arguments, mustering evidence about appropriate size to support their own interests.

She goes on to indicate how incompletely founded are the views on size of administrative unit that are regularly advocated in educational debate, noting that they spring largely from partisan political and professional sources:

The review of the political controversy over the size of unit for educational administration revealed many of the contradictory claims that have been made. In essence the claims for small units have been directed at the participatory aspects for citizen influence over decision-making seeing education mainly as consumption. Larger units, in the context of this argument, are seen as being unresponsive to the needs of the local community and, where tried, too bureaucratic, not allowing for popular control. Rather a professional control has developed in which either the teachers or the administrators are seen as having decisive influence. Thus the arguments for small size of unit come from groups in society that have been excluded from access to decision-making.

The demand for large units comes from an entirely different set of interests and with different objectives in mind. Here the need for an efficient organization, purveying a quality system of education for society's investment, is seen as paramount. A larger unit is necessary to obtain the financial and economic resources for this purpose and in the long run is cheaper because of economics of scale. Also a large unit may allow for diversity in educational offerings. The main protagonists of these arguments have been either the politicians presently in control of the system or the professionals, either teachers or administrators, who thereby extend their influence over the system.

Research evidence, notably that of Coleman (1966) and Jencks (1972), suggests that David is correct; that here as in much of the ecological debate we have a very unclear view of the consequences of differential ecological environments. Some positive results have indeed been thrown up. For instance, the first NFER study (Monks, 1968) on comprehensive schools suggested that pupils in small schools scored higher on tests of reading, mathematical and non-verbal ability than those in larger schools. But the significance was little more than marginal and the findings heavily qualified. David's review of this and subsequent NFER research (Monks, 1968, 1970), the work of Benn and Simon (1970) and a long catalogue of other workers suggests a similar pattern of largely inconclusive findings. The agnostic conclusions she reaches leads her to advocate research which 'would benefit from being directed to the analysis of concrete events and processes rather than the chimerical pursuit of eternal constancies of educational organization artificially abstracted from this historical context, and used as prescriptive statements.'

The response of the individual

In view of the extreme difficulty that arises from attempts to relate specific rather than general ecological factors to educational attainments, the conclusions of Byrne, Williamson and Fletcher seem to rest at least to some extent on a generalized act of faith.

The danger in assuming that the school has little impact on differences in results is that differences then have to be accounted for in terms of the attributes of individuals. The general conclusion sustained by our findings is that school system inputs are of considerable importance in explaining differences in attainment. In addition, there is a systematic relationship between the class background of an area and the educational resources available.

Not surprisingly, Byrne, Williamson and Fletcher, like all writers so far cited in this chapter, place heavy emphasis on the ecology of educational systems or institutions rather than on the educational ecology of the individuals. Yet it is clear that if we are to go beyond the generalized statements and attempt to provide usable information for teachers and administrators we must focus our attention more sharply on the behaviour of individuals. This too will help to avoid the perennial danger of the ecological fallacy – the attribution of uniform behaviour to statistical aggregates. It is also imperative to rediscover the individual if we are to take advantage of the insights of the interpretative approaches introduced in the previous chapter. In particular it will allow us to further investigate the capacity of the individual to invest his ecological environment with interpretations which in a real sense modify its characteristics for him. Barker and Gump (1964), the doyens of investigations on school size and attainment in North America, early discovered the importance of this 'subjective' fact. They write: 'There is indeed an inside-outside perceptual paradox, a school size illusion. ... Small high schools are, in fact, not so small on the inside as on the outside.'

The response to compensatory programmes

But perhaps the greatest incentive to rediscover the individual arose out of the disillusion over the very large American compensatory programmes of the mid 1960s, notably the national pre-school programme Head Start. Such projects had been based upon the simple belief that substantially enhanced educational provision could, by leading to enhanced attainment, compensate for a socio-economic environment deemed to be inferior. The Westinghouse report on Head Start (Cicirellie, 1969) showed, however, that the project had had no substantial lasting effect on the intellectual and social development of those children who had experienced it. Hawkridge (1968) had already found that these same strictures were indeed generally true of all projects up to that time.

Yet Halsey (1972) in his review of the American programmes was able to identify a small number where effective intervention had taken place. In all of these, the individual participants had come to take a new view of the educational resources available to them, had in some way redefined their relationship to them and to their own socio-economic environment and in such ways had come to respond differently to them. Essentially such programmes had led individuals to redefine themselves as part of the network of educational resources – as aides, auxiliaries either in liaison with the teachers or by creating an additional set of educational resources outside the schools (Poster, 1971). Others have developed parental involvement through home visiting schemes and teaching in the homes in which parents participated. Still others, notably those advocated in Britain by Midwinter (1974), had involved substantial community participation taking the form of bringing school staff into close relationship with members of the community and vice versa. In some cases this involved a measurable degree of closer community control over the school. In some it involved using the community itself as an educational resource – notably in the Philadelphia Parkway School which, with no building of its own, used the community as classroom – its museums, workshops, council chambers, streets, shops and parks.

An important consideration of many community oriented projects has been to challenge the distribution between the socio-economic and the educational resources that is commonly made, to see them and the response to them as a total ecological scene. Halsey writes:

> However, it would be foolish to underestimate the difficulties in the way of establishing such a community school. Experience has shown that community schools in working class areas have often failed because of the narrow, formal and traditional approach adopted by those in charge. The community side of such schools is often nothing more than the ordinary further education centre attached to the existing school building. Parents have little say in the running of such centres nor in the activities offered for their benefit.
>
> The community school must be prepared to listen to parents, to advise and assist, rather than tell 'them' what 'we' think they should do. Community and social workers have learnt this lesson, and adult educationalists must do likewise. This is no easy task. It may mean a new type of professional, a Community Adult Educationalist attached to community schools.

The essence of the American situation seems to be that differences in educational provision only work when the individual sees them and his situation in a new way, when effectively his identity within his total ecological structure is changed:

> To simplify our description of American compensatory education programmes we can say that the movement began with what appeared to be a simple educational problem, the fact that certain social groups on average had a lower level of educational performance. Attempts to solve that problem were forced to go further and further outside the educational system, as the ramifications of the initial problem were uncovered. In this process the most basic questions are raised about the nature of social organization, and about the reasons why lower status should be associated with lower educational performance. These developments indicate that a purely educational response to the initial problem is unlikely to succeed. Action programmes have tended to follow this pattern, first seeking to introduce changes in the child's experience in the formal school setting, and then increasingly to widen their approach, so that larger areas of the child's experience are affected. Educational underachievement has become merely one manifestation of a series of social and economic disparities experienced by disadvantaged groups. The long-term solution must be a comprehensive policy which strikes at these political, social and economic inequalities.

Response and ecological change

Yet, as we shall discuss in the final chapter, changed perception may be insufficient to effect a redistribution of attainment. We may also need to consider the prospect of a change in the eco-structure itself and, in part, the prospect of a change in the power structure. Halsey anticipates this:

> It is possible, too, that educational programmes may make considerable impact on the political consciousness of the poor, a process that has certainly accompanied the development of compensatory education in the United States. Such political awakening may be the most effective means of ensuring that the gross inequalities between social and ethnic groups are eradicated.

Robinson (1976) in his review of interventionist strategies takes a similarly quietly optimistic view. He draws attention to the small but encouraging evidence, not only of 'early gains' in attainment but also of the isolated but firm evidence of the persistence of those gains.

In Britain, as in the United States, there are encouraging signs that the new realistic appreciations of the complex relationships between provision and response, along with the sensitive techniques needed to investigate them, are becoming established within the educational system. Certainly the initiation of two new units by the Department of Education and Science in England and Wales is an encouraging step. One is the Educational Development Unit led by Clegg which is specially concerned with the exploration of provision and response of children whose low existing response to provision seems to spring from social disadvantage. The other is the Assessment of Performance Unit led by senior members of the Inspectorate which is taking a broader but equally detailed view of the link between provision and response throughout the school system. Both units, as an important part of their work, will be obliged to consider not only response but also the definition of what is seen to be acceptable response – a definition that in itself is susceptible to change in the light of the interventionists strategies and the political consequences which Halsey has referred to. Certainly an important part of the early work of the Assessment of Performance Unit has been to explore the definitions of acceptable attainment at primary and secondary schools.

The socially mixed school

The Educational Priority Project had as its *raison d'être* the establishment of policies and practice for priority schools in priority areas. But the redistribution of educational resources may be attempted through other strategies. A long established strategy is through the socially mixed school where it is assumed that not only will children from all social backgrounds have the same access to resources but also, because of the presence of children and parents who know how to demand, use and respond to resources effectively, those who would not otherwise do so fully will come to do so. For example, in the intake class of a modern infants school in an egalitarian inspired education authority favouring mixed catchment areas one is likely to find children from a wide range of social backgrounds in a well equipped modern classroom, well stocked with early learning equipment. This is likely to be of the kind supplied by well-known firms such as Galt and

Abbatt, firms well known not only to education authorities but also to middle class families who will commonly have such equipment available in the home. Usually too they will have attitudes to its use and to early learning in general that are cognate with those of the teacher (Bernstein and Young, 1967). With such a nucleus of children familiar with the equipment and its purposes, it is argued that the others will soon learn how. It may also be argued that through contact between the parents the message about its import and purpose would also be transmitted.

Barnes, a former member of the London team of the Educational Priority Project, has explored such expectations which came to be closely linked with those of the Educational Priority Project (1977). Yet here again, as Barnes reminds us, there is little evidence either way that illuminates the effectiveness of these rather simple educational strategies. Implicit in his account is a view that more depends on the patterns of individual perception and interpretation. Certainly it is clear from Barnes's comments that the view that social mix can effect the take-up of education resources by a simple contagion process is as naive as some of the early ecological engineering strategies that assumed that resources had only to be distributed to be taken up effectively.

It may even be that the consequences are the reverse of what was intended. King, in a study of comprehensive schools in a local education authority (1974), noted that schools with working class catchment areas were associated with lower levels of attainment than those with middle class catchment areas. Yet the local education authority in this area as in others had provided more generous pupil–teacher ratios for the working class schools. Some examination opportunities were also more generously available and staff stability was higher. Though King draws attention to other administrative variables, for example a policy of short course comprehensive schooling that almost certainly had some bearing on the situation, his paper nonetheless offers a further rebuttal of any simple monocausal link between provision and attainment.

Conclusion

The list of researchers who conclude either despondently or triumphantly, depending upon their personal ideology, that a clear link between provision and response cannot be established is endless. Their research has covered not only general environment and size and staffing but also curriculum and teaching methodology. Much of the evidence was assembled by Averech (1972) who concluded, 'The research on teaching approaches, teacher difference, class size and the like shows no consistent effect on student achievement as measured by standard cognitive tests.'

Yet examination of the research under review suggests that most of the inquiries have hypothesized the crude causality that we have discussed on several occasions in this chapter. Yet where more sensitive, individually oriented explorations have taken place, for the most part since Averech's study, there is clear indication (as Halsey and Robinson have shown) that changes in provision have effected changes in response and demand, and equally importantly that the reverse has also occurred. But what is equally clear is that provision and response can never be treated as isolated variables; they are both inextricably entwined, not independent but dependent on the totality of the ecological environment of the society and of the individual. With hindsight it is clear that a great deal of ecological research is probably no more realistic than a project on, say, travelling on the school bus which set out to prove that the repeated experience made children more enthusiastic to become bus drivers. Tyler (1977) writes strikingly but perceptively on this matter:

> What is the meaning of a statement which connects the number of books in a library with points on reading tests? What has happened to individual care, patience and love in this discussion of 'quality'? The only answer is that *of course* personal warmth, affection and humour do matter for cognitive growth, and can never be quantified as any input or output. Education is not simply about reading scores and 'beta' co-efficients in a statistical model. The only trouble has been that policy makers and professionals of all kinds in the past often mentally added 'bad schools' to 'poor homes' and came up with 'dumb kids'. They have therefore deduced that having better schools will show up the other side of the equation. If the statistical game is worth anything it has undermined this kind of reasoning.

Jencks (1972), like most of his colleagues, shows himself well aware of these dangers. He sees educational resources as important but, like any other area of social provision, marginal. In consequence he points out the almost self-evident truth – that public policy, if it wishes to tackle inequality or any other social problem, should do so directly rather than by 'leaving it to the schools' or any other institution. Indeed he argues, rather like Bowles and Gintis (1977) have done subsequently, that 'leaving it to the schools' is something of a public conspiracy; that attempting to alleviate human inequality by providing more education is a kind of politically acceptable method of guilt alleviation. It is a method that hides the necessity for doing something about the social system as a whole, even though this is the fundamental cause of the inequality.

For this reason alone the popular verdict on Jencks's work – that it shows that education doesn't make any difference – is wrong but the verdict is also wrong in another special and important sense. Jencks, like Little and Westergaard (1964) and Boudon (1973), shows that education normally plays a very important part indeed in reinforcing the existing social structure, the distribution of roles and power within it ensuring (to use Bourdieu's terms) the cultural and social reproduction of society.

Here again we see ecology as a study of the realities of social life, not a private instrument for those who wish to examine change any more than it is the property of those who wish only to examine social class.

In reaching this conclusion, we have gone some way to supporting Byrne, Williamson and Fletcher's advocacy of educational provision as a causal factor. Yet we have reached this position by seeing it as a far less sharply defined factor than they have and also through the individual analyses that they have rejected. A more appropriate position for Byrne, Williamson and Fletcher may have been to reject the inadequacies of the predominantly crude individual analyses available to them rather than to reject individually oriented interactional and interpretative analyses as a genre. Potentially, and to some extent even at present, such analyses offer a more convincing confirmation of the importance of educational resources than the complex statistical procedures have been used as an alternative to them.

Summary

We commenced this chapter with a review of the evidence of the response to the provision of education, paying particular attention to Byrne, Williamson and Fletcher's argument that this evidence showed causality rather than mere correlation. But the difficulties of the group analyses used by them and most other investigators led us to reconsider the relevance of the responses and particularly the interpretations of individuals that had been first mentioned in the previous chapter. Using such evidence, particularly that generated in the British Educational Priority Project, we have outlined a modest but optimistic support for the existence of a positive link between educational provision and response. But this is seen to be a link that exists within the total ecology of the social system and the total ecological background of the individual.

4

The process of ecological distribution

In the previous chapter we considered the distribution of education and the distribution of the response to which it gives rise. But we have not yet considered the ways in which the distribution of education occurs, the ways in which resources are allocated within and between the parts of the system. How is the class-teacher ratio determined at a local as well as a national level? In what circumstances may a school be expanded, maintained or even closed? Why do capitation allowances vary between different types of secondary schools or different ages of pupils? How are the rules established for the secondment of teachers, for determining the appointment of school counsellors and the purchase of laboratory equipment?

The national scene

In the educational system in Britain, as in most others, the parameters for such decisions are laid down at a national level. Governmental policies on such global matters as economic development, the redistribution of income, the alleviation of poverty and even foreign policy, constitute a framework within which the total resources of education and the priorities to which they are to be directed are determined. Initiatives taken within central bureaux such as, in Britain, the Cabinet and the Treasury, are passed on to national educational administrations which not only execute such policies but also play an important part in determining them and a still more important part in interpreting them whilst they are executing them. With the educational administration the key decisions will be taken by a small group of senior administrative civil servants. For England and Wales, Kogan (1975) has estimated that this group comprises some sixty officers.

In Britain in the 1970s there have, as always, been many examples of the interplay of general and specifically educational policies with visible implications for the distribution of resources. Government commitment to egalitarianism has, amongst other strategies, given rise to a policy of comprehensive secondary schooling which has in turn led the Department of Education and Science to develop strategies which increased the share of resources available to comprehensive schools and reduced that available to grammar schools, notably through the use of powers to control the approval of building plans (though, at the time of writing, there is no direct legislative power to compel the introduction of comprehensive schools as the 'Tameside dispute' made clear when a local authority was able to resist government pressure to reorganize its secondary schools). The decline of the birth rate and the economic pressures to reduce government spending caused the central government to call upon the Department of Education and Science to revise its estimates of the future size of the teaching profession, to reduce the flow of resources to initial teacher training and to implement a programme of closure or reduction of teacher training institutions.

The rate support grant

Notwithstanding the complexity of the paths and the multitude of competing claims, the history of the national provision of resources for education has been one of continuing rise, both relative and absolute, for almost three decades from 1945. Vaizey and Sheehan (1968) noted that expenditure on education rose from 12·9 per cent of public expenditure in the mid 1950s to 18·9 per cent in the mid 1960s; from 3·2 per cent of the GNP in the mid 1950s to 5 per cent in the mid 1960s. In 1974 it was estimated that education consumed some 6 per cent of the GNP. Though comparative figures for the mid 1970s are not available at the time of writing it is unlikely, despite the public spending cuts of the 1970s, that educational spending has significantly declined relative to other public expenditure. The extent of central government control over local education authorities is exercised to a large extent through the working of the *rate support grant*.

The calculation of the rate support grant is complex, involving, in addition to the size of the services provided by local authorities, calculation of 'need' to enable poorer authorities to reach national average standards and a range of subsidy payments made to individuals and households through local authorities. The grant is negotiated each December for the following financial year. In 1976–7 this met 65·5 per cent of all local authority expenditure; for 1977–8 the proportion was reduced to 61 per cent. Though the rate support grant is a block grant covering the whole of local authority expenditure – including such diverse matters as social services, buses and public housing – education accounts for by far the greater share – 49 per cent in 1975–6.

The power of the central government arises from the changes in rate support grant it imposes upon local authorities. Faced with a cut in grant a local authority has for the most part two alternatives – to increase local revenue raising, usually through rate increases, or to decrease expenditure. Both are courses likely to present political hazards to the ruling party. Education as the largest item in the budget is therefore inescapably subject to political considerations: the process of resource allocation cannot be other than a substantially political process.

There is abundant evidence of the use by central government of the rate support grant instrument to control public spending, particularly in education. After the boom years of the 1950s and 1960s when the growth in expenditure on education continued in an almost unbroken rise, the first major cut in educational spending was announced shortly after the publication of the government white paper *Education: A Framework for Expansion* (Cmnd. 5174) in December 1973. These involved a reduction of £182 million in 1974–5, mainly at the expense of planned new buildings but also including a cut of £63 million in 'procurements' – books, materials and other equipment. Further cuts were announced in November 1974, again via the rate support grant calculation. Circular 12/74 contained the words 'Local authorities are asked for each service to limit their plans only to what is strictly necessary to meet inescapable commitments.'

In 1975 Circular 10/75 announced a standstill in educational spending growth and recommended the following course of action to local authorities:

1 First priority for available resources should be for pupils within the compulsory age range – the aim being to maintain but not to improve standards.
2 Uneconomical groups of students in the 16–19 group should be avoided.
3 In higher education additional students should be accommodated within existing resources.
4 Rising fives should not be admitted unless they make no additional call on educational resources and do not prevent the redeployment of those resources for more essential purposes.

The standstill was confirmed in the rate support grant announced in November 1975 of £480 million. In February the government published *Public Expenditure to 1979–80* (Cmnd. 6393) indicating that planned expenditure in education would be cut by £1000 million in the next three years, £84 million in 1976–77, £331 million in 1977–78, £618 million in 1978–79. Education was to be required to carry 25 per cent of the total reduction in expenditure. In November 1976, as we have already mentioned, the rate support grant was reduced by a further 4·5 per cent. Though the impact of the rate support grant on all local authorities is substantial, it is far greater on the less wealthy authorities. E. M. Byrne (1976) writes:

Authorities fall roughly into three categories, those which are financially wealthy, those which have rate resources at about the national average and those which are well below average. The first may enjoy some degree of political and financial freedom, since they are likely to retain a *development* budget of excess financial resources, over and above that needed to carry out their statutory duties. Moreover, an analysis of the product of a 1p rate for authorities after local government organization shows that those with *high rate yield* happen also to be those with *low social need* on the whole, predominantly middle class areas with high quality housing, low school population, good transport and a high provision of sixth form and tertiary places. The second category, average authority, will in most normal years be able to maintain its past policies and standards even if the Department restricts expansion. However, the third category of LEAs, with resources below the national average, is dependent on very substantial *rate support grant* in order even to pay basic salaries, to maintain schools and colleges and to administer the authority. *RSG does not give a margin for development.* These LEAs are therefore especially dependent upon the fluctuations of the political climate at the time of RSG negotiations each autumn. An example of the latter was the unforeseen decision in 1973 crudely to swing priority to urban areas by recalculating the formula base for RSG, which resulted in practice in unexpected cuts of the order of £5 million a year in government grant for some rural counties. Since this was well beyond any predictable level of annual fluctuation, treasurers and CEOs of those areas were faced in late November with urgent decisions for the complete re-allocation of their budget for the following April in order to preserve essential services.

Though Byrne is offering further emphasis of the importance of central government control, her illustration neatly illustrates the way in which the actual decisions about resource planning and expenditure still fall to the local education authority. For a wealthy authority a coherent resource policy is feasible; for an impoverished one faced with short notice fluctuations in RSG it can at least be expedient and opportunist. Yet both authorities are held to be equally responsible by central government and by their constituents for the educational ecology of the area they serve.

A number of published documents offer guidance to the complex paths through which central government decisions are reached. These range from the White Papers on Public Expenditure published in January each year through to the various reports and circulars to which we have already referred. These paths involve a mixture of rationality and carefully assembled evidence, political expediency and opportunism, personal interest and the effects of pressure groups and, ultimately, the will of the electorate. Several notable guides through the labyrinth exist. Bernbaum (1967) usefully reviews the period from 1918 to 1944. The story is continued by Vaizey's *The Control of Education* (1963). Another guide is Kogan's *Educational Policy Making* (1975) which reviews the development of major policy trends and their consequences in the period 1960–74. This volume explains in detail the striking proliferation of national pressure groups in the

1960s – bodies such as the Comprehensive Schools Association, the Advisory Centre for Education and many more – and the effective way they and the longer established groups have played a part in the development of national policy. Of particular interest to the interpretative analysis introduced in earlier chapters in his conclusion on the range of perspectives from which policy is viewed:

> Any single policy takes on multiple guises and is viewed differently at many points of a complex system: pupils, teachers, the head, the chief education officer and his administrative and advisory staffs, councillors, the local electorate, the national electorate, Parliament, the DES, researchers, journalists, teacher educators, the churches, employers and the trade unions.

Ministerial reminiscences such as those of Crossman (1975, 1976) often provide more illuminating lights than official documents. In education a particularly helpful *entré* to central decision making strategies is offered in *The Politics of Education* (Boyle, Crosland and Kogan, 1971) where two former Secretaries of State for Education (ministers) recall the ways in which governmental policies and decisions on the size and distribution of education resources emerged in the 1960s. They offer further evidence of the complex but important ways in which the personal preferences of the incumbent Minister of Education can influence this distribution – affecting its size, speed and destination.

A particularly important feature of the distribution of educational resources at a national level in Britain are the officially appointed Advisory Councils and Committees. It is only when one considers the existence of these bodies and their chairman and individual members that one can begin to explain the origins and impetus of many of the policy decisions that have had profound consequences for the distribution of educational resources. It would be difficult, for instance, to explain fully the widespread emphasis on child centred education in British primary schools without reference to such bodies, particularly the Plowden Committee. The development of the concept of Educational Priority Areas also owes much to that Committee and the personal advocacy of the Chairman herself. The Bullock Committee (1975) on the experience of language, with its powerful affirmation of the importance of reading, has had an unquestionable effect in ensuring that a considerably greater proportion of education resources are devoted to the teaching of reading than would otherwise be the case. The aphorism 'universal decisions are made by individuals' is unmistakably true in education.

But it is not only the formal specialist committee that formulates policy on education. There is an extensive set of informal channels peopled not so much by pressure groups as by members of the 'educational establishment' as Boyle, Crosland and Kogan describe. Boyle writes about the source of policies: 'this is the difference between education and some other subject. I would say overwhelmingly the biggest number originated from the "education world".' This would include not only the leading personnel of the national pressure groups but also the more influential chief education officers, teachers, academics and educational journalists.

The local authority scene

It is unquestionably true that macro-decisions, reached through central government, play a great part, arguably the major part, in the process of resource allocation in Britain. Yet by far the greater part of the precise determination of policy and its execution occurs at a local level. It is here that the resources are assembled and made available to those who will use them. The boundary line between national and local decision making is one that is seldom clearly drawn and is keenly fought over. In the Callaghan initiated debate on educational standards in 1976, newspaper headlines reflected both the fluidity and contentiousness of the frontier. Within a few days, 'Ministry seeks greater control of the use of our schools' was followed by 'Local authorities resist extension of government interference in their schools'.

The Times Educational Supplement of 19 November 1976 reported that:

Whitehall will be given direct control over part of the money spent on education if Mrs Shirley Williams, Secretary of State for Education, has her way.

In an interview with the *TES* this week Mrs Williams spelt out more clearly than she has before her wish to see the law changed to allow some direct funding (specific grants) of education by her Department. At present virtually all of the money for education is paid to local authorities in the form of rate support grant.

The report goes on to surmise: 'The local authority associations are not likely to welcome guidance from Mrs Williams on how they should spend the rate support grant money. They will be particularly hostile if the rate support grant is reduced overall.'

Notwithstanding the outcome of the debate, however, it is clear that, in the foreseeable future the distribution of resources will, as Chapter 2 has shown, be critically determined by the local education authorities. In the light of this, the main focus of this volume must be the more detailed local study of the ecology of education that exists within overall government strategies: to explain the local processes that lead to considerable unevenness between and even within a single education system – unevennesses that have been strikingly in evidence in the two previous chapters of this book. Undoubtedly one of the best ways to probe the process of distribution is to look at the ways in which local education authorities make decisions – ways that have already been implicit in our earlier considerations. It is now time to make them explicit.

A number of studies, predominantly American, directly examined the working of local education administrators. Most made the now predictable link between decision making and the socio-economic status of the area served. Minar (1966) related variations in the style and content of the decision making process of school systems (local education authorities) serving areas with different socio-economic structures, those of 'high status and low social conflict' and those with 'low status and high social conflict'. The high status, low conflict areas had administrations which dealt with resource allocation and other decisions with fewer formal procedures and wider discretionary powers for the superintendent. Policy discussions focused more on curricular than financial issues. Precisely opposite practices characterized the low status, high conflict areas.

One of the most detailed explorations of the way in which the local situation affects administrative behaviour is in Nicholas's (1965) study of the day to day working of an elementary school office, which indicates an almost total determination of decisions by factors arising from the local area including its political and ideological traditions.

The diffusion and imprecision of the goals of educational organization render them and their personnel particularly liable to external pressure. The analysis of educational administration is unlikely to be adequate or even meaningful unless due attention is given to these; the often limited attention that such pressures receive in analyses of administrative systems generally is likely to be particularly disadvantageous in studies in this field. In Britain there has been rather less attempt to look at the context of educational administration. The less powerful position of local elected representatives on this side of the Atlantic and the way in which, in Britain, representatives serve as a shield to protect the professional education service (both administrators and teachers) from much of the impact of external local pressures may partly account for this neglect. As Baron and Howell (1968) and Jennings (1977) have pointed out, the school administration in Britain is largely insulated from direct but not indirect social pressures concerning the distribution of resources.

Yet in Britain, as in America, educational administrations face a similar framework within which decisions must be made. This is the division of resources into three broad categories – teaching staff salaries, non-teaching staff salaries, and equipment and materials. Of these, the first is much the largest, usually some four times greater than the others combined, and increasing proportionately as teachers become more successful in negotiating salary rises. Equipment and materials, on the other hand, seldom exceed 10 per cent of local education budgets on either side of the Atlantic. And even within these proportions the amount of effective choice is also limited. Briault (1974), in a useful introductory account of the allocation and management of resources, has shown how predetermined, in the short run, is much of the resource distribution of local education authorities by existing commitments.

Examining the local authority

Perhaps the simplest way to understand local decision making on resources lies in the case study technique which reviews a set of administrative decisions in the local context. Though such studies are still rare, there are several examples which have looked at secondary reorganization in English local education authority areas. Saran (1973) has undertaken a detailed study of policy making in secondary education in 'Townley', tracing the sequence of policy phases and successive reorganizations of the various secondary schools in the local authority and the roles of the decision making personnel since 1948. E. M. Byrne (1974) has analysed resource allocation in three local education authorities

– Lincoln, Nottingham and Northumberland – with particular emphasis on the demand for provision experienced by the authorities. She reports that neither explicit demand (such as that from influential bodies) or implicit demand (such as that from rising numbers) were significantly influential. She also emphasizes what has already been demonstrated in this chapter, that 'the financial system exists in almost total dissociation from needs and problems'.

Two further studies will be considered here, those undertaken at Croydon and Northamptonshire by Donnison and Chapman (1965) and Eggleston (1974b). Both used a pattern of interviews which involved personnel and studied official documentation, newspaper reports and other local commentaries to analyse the influence of established and specially created pressure groups such as parent-teacher associations, political and religious organizations, old pupils' associations and the like, and also the unstructured and largely informal pressures exercised by individuals using local media of communication. Both studies identify a very considerable degree of effective pressure on the local authority's decision making role.

Donnison and Chapman's study is of the preparation of plans for reorganization of a group of long established secondary schools which, during the period under review, failed to reach fruition, due not only to the conflict between advocates of change and conservatism but also to the conflict within both groups of advocates. They identify a number of familiar features of the administrative situation:

> The initial recognition of stresses calling for reappraisal of the system, the formulation of different – and sometimes conflicting – interpretations of this situation among groups with divergent frames of reference, the involvement of a widening circle of interests capable of exercising influence on the decisions to be made, and the concentration of pressures focused upon the body responsible for those decisions.

The way in which the actions of the professional administrator are both precipitated by and subsequently modified by the interplay of local factors is clearly shown, as is the way in which such factors can override the 'rationality' of 'pure' administrative behaviour. However, as Donnison and Chapman suggest in their conclusion, it is possible for the strength of the contextual factors to be intensified by the professional 'providers' of the service:

When important groups among those providing the service suffer, or expect to suffer, a serious loss of resources, powers or status, conflicts arise among them which will spread, if pressed sufficiently far, to a widening circle of outside interests capable of influencing the development of the service. The timing of decisions about this development then calls for sensitive judgement. For premature attempts to resolve such conflicts may commit those responsible for these decisions to standpoints which provoke unnecessarily intransigent opposition among those who must eventually play a part in the evolution of the service. Major participants in this evolution may then be compelled to resign, or evolution itself may be brought to a halt.

Eggleston's study is of plans to reorganize secondary education in a Northamptonshire new town where a conventional but only recently established pattern of selective secondary schools existed. Here the contextual pressures were polarized not so much into those for and against change but those for greater or lesser degrees of change. Partly because this distinction was not reflected by existing pressure groups, and partly because of the relatively unstructured nature of the new town population, the pressures were at first diffuse and fragmentary. But the study shows a remarkably rapid restructuring of the local community around new organizations – the militant left wing Association for Comprehensive Education standing for fundamental change and the *ad hoc* committee of teachers favouring only modest change. The pattern of events was one in which, for a time, control seemed to have passed out of the hands of the local education authority. Having a firm and politically inescapable commitment to reorganize secondary education, it found itself without a detailed plan and with widespread opposition to its tentative proposals. Faced with this situation the authority turned to the *ad hoc* committee which determined the arrangements ultimately adopted. The *ad hoc* committee thereby effectively determined the crucial allocation of resources for secondary education. Yet though in the period under review the *ad hoc* committee emerged triumphant, it is to be noted that, as in the Croydon study, there is no final resolution of the conflicting contextual pressures, merely a new and transitory equilibrium.

Saran (1973), presenting a further study of comprehensive reorganization in 'Townley', written in the context of a wider

75

analysis of educational policies in the area, reaches a similar conclusion. She writes:

> The impetus for change certainly does not come from any single group in society. It is a complex process, and the changing views of some participants fertilize those of others. Decisions about changes in policy and in administrative practice are closely related to changes in informed opinion. Indeed, these two factors reinforce each other.

Models of resource allocation

Following the case studies of administrative behaviour we may construct macro- and micro-models of administrative behaviour. The macro approach is usefully reviewed in *Handbook of Statistical Needs for Educational Investment Planning* (OECD, 1966) and offers a valuable survey of the range of contextual inputs for which allowance must be made in the construction of macro-models. The possibilities of study of this kind are clearly to be seen in the work of Stone (1965), who sets out a long term model of the total education system of England and Wales which brings together the human inputs into the system – namely the flows of students through its various branches – and the economic inputs – the costs of teachers, buildings and equipment. A focal point of the analysis is the 'decision spectrum' occurring at the point of the minimum school leaving age. In a subsequent article, Stone (1966) contrasts and compares the structure of both types of input and uses his results to examine the problems of time lag and demographic flow using output as well as the more usual input coefficients for the latter problems. As Stone notes, at this stage the analysis of the education system has become but a part of the analysis of the demographic system at large and the analysis of economic inputs to the education system has become a part of the analysis of the productive system at large.

At the 'macro' level a number of organizational analyses of educational resource allocation have been attempted. Such a model built around a small specific administrative act is that of Mood (1967) who portrays the issues surrounding a decision to use films as an aid to teaching high school biology courses, and in doing so demonstrates the role of such an analysis in bringing to light unconscious and untested assumptions of the school administrators in making resources available. It offers an

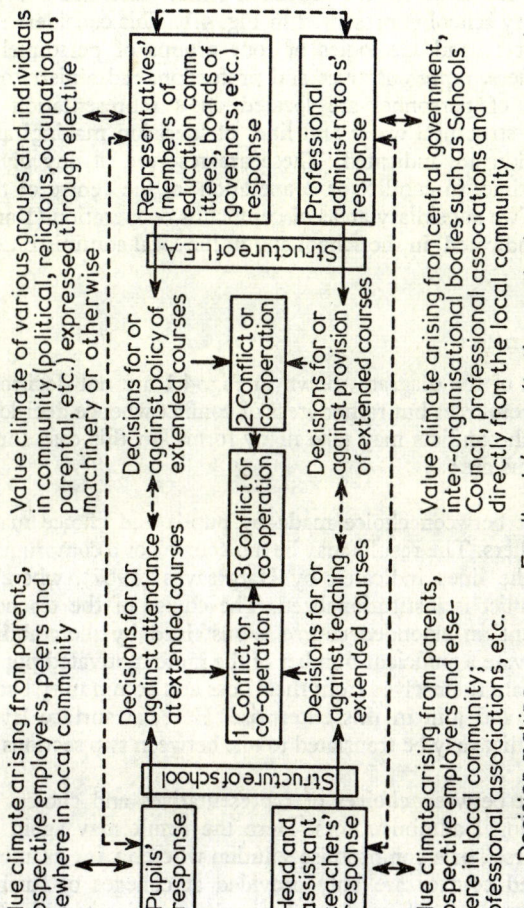

Fig. 4.1 *Resource allocation procedure: provision of new facilities for extended courses in a secondary school*

Value climate of various groups and individuals in community (political, religious, occupational, parental, etc.) expressed through elective machinery or otherwise

Representatives' (members of education committees, boards of governors, etc.) response

Professional administrators' response

Structure of L.E.A.

Decisions for or against policy of extended courses

Decisions for or against provision of extended courses

2 Conflict or co-operation

3 Conflict or co-operation

1 Conflict or co-operation

Value climate arising from central government, inter-organisational bodies such as Schools Council, professional associations and directly from the local community

Decisions for or against attendance at extended courses

Decisions for or against teaching extended courses

Structure of school

Pupils' response

Head and assistant teachers' response

Value climate arising from parents, prospective employers, peers and elsewhere in local community

Value climate arising from parents, prospective employers and elsewhere in local community; professional associations, etc.

——— Decision making   ------- Feedback (consultation and other communication)

attractive means of bringing together the process of resource allocation so far reviewed.

A model of the decision making procedure associated with the allocation of resources for the provision of new extended courses in a secondary school is presented in Fig. 4.1. This considers the values, climates and ideologies of four groups of personnel – pupils, teachers, representatives and professional administrators. The groups of personnel are located on a representation of the relevant structural order and lines of 'decision making' and communication are indicated. These are resolved at any given moment of time, in conflict or cooperation, at the centre of the model (3). Two subsidiary areas of conflict or cooperation (1 and 2) are also indicated, in the school and in the local administration respectively.

Areas of conflict

At the heart of the diagram shown in Fig. 4.1 are not decisions concerning resources but rather areas of conflict whence decisions emerge. Such conflicts may take many forms. In this case three possible forms are:

1 Conflict between choice made by pupils and choice made by teachers. The results may be 'no course', or a compromise along the lines indicated by Hargreaves (1967), whereby the conflict is institutionalized. The choice of the teachers to mount an extended course is sustained by their ability to motivate a sufficient number of the more motivated pupils to alienate themselves from their peer and community background and join in this enterprise. Here, at surface level, the conflict may be translated to one between two sections of pupils.

2 Conflict between choices of representatives and choices of professional administrators. Here the result may again be 'no course', or a compromise solution whereby, for example, extended courses are only provided at colleges of further education or at a few selected schools involving transfer for the majority of pupils. The need to transfer between schools in order to obtain further education introduces an element of social selection, as we have seen students with substantial home support for continued education are likely to transfer readily. Those who rely on peer support for continued

bove and beyond the introduction of new examination re-
ents. The established pattern of examinations itself consti-
e of the major determinants of the distribution of resources
secondary schools. No education authority and no school
ightly expose itself to the charge that it had placed its stu-
hances of success at risk by failing to provide the necessary
es at a level that was at least adequate. And, as we have
tempts to limit the number of students seeking entry to
examinations are likely to be frustrated. The combination
ination requirements and student demand constitutes a
y unchallengeable case for resource allocation. And, as
e Schools Council and every other decision making body,
mining boards too are surrounded by a plethora of interest
notably those of the teachers, which are often represented
committee structure.

litical parties

interest groups are active throughout the resource al-
processes of the British system, they are specific. Though
able to focus attention on issues and obtain spectacular
t is usually narrowly based and short lived. The enduring
rpose influential pressures emanate not from interest
ut from the political parties. In each one or other of
es – usually Conservative and Labour, and, in Scotland
les, also Nationalist, along with a range of minority
rules, sometimes in coalition, more usually alone. The
sk of the parties, locally as well as nationally, is to win
– hopefully with a clear majority – and so take control
olitical decisions including education. The allocation
ces for education in this case becomes susceptible to
party's philosophy. Here the ideological component
been implicit in other areas of influence becomes

ature of the British party system ensures the primacy
rty over all other local influences. Jennings (1976)

lization of other sources of influence on policy making
for the controlling party. This takes three directions.
r protection and easy legislation, access to the policy
is restricted by taking control of those parts of the local

education are less likely to do so. In such circumstances the
conflict may again, at a surface level, be seen as one between
two sections of the student body. Or it may be translated
into a conflict between the secondary and further educational
establishments or between the two categories of secondary
school.

3 Conflict between the school and the professional administrative sectors. Again the result is likely to be an institutionalization of conflict. This may take a number of forms in which
existing or new organizations are brought in. For instance,
the conflict may be formalized between, on the one hand
parent-teacher associations, teachers' associations, teachers'
organizations, associations for the advancement of state
education, and, on the other, denominational groups, political parties, and professional administrators. Or it may involve specially created organizations to preserve or to
promote extended education such as local action groups,
refurbished old pupils' associations or pupil organizations.
An early example of this was the 'school strike' at Gosford
Hill School, Oxfordshire, in 1959, where an organization
of pupils formed to resist the arrangements of the LEA
that extended courses should be established at other secondary schools but not that one.

The conflict may take forms and these forms go a considerable
way to explain the quite different administrative climates of local
education authorities – some open and accessible in their dealings,
not only for their employees but also with teachers, parents and
children, others faceless and defended in their actions, with
'closed' education committee meetings and closed membership
of governing bodies or, in the case of the school, by limited
parental access and closed professional ranks, all designed to meet
the challenge from outside.

Byrne and Williamson (1972), in their study of educational
provision in North East England, consider two policy models of
local authorities. One is 'the elite oriented authority model in
which resources are differentially concentrated on the sponsored
elite with consequent high attainment of this elite'. The other is
'the egalitarian authority model where resources are more evenly
spread throughout the school system with consequent 'inferior'
attainment of an elitist kind but where the evidence suggests that
there is a higher overall attainment of total school populations.'

governmental structure open to non-elected members of the public. Second, there is a sorting out of who will be heard, when and under what circumstances. Third, strategies are devised for dealing with requests and parcelling out information, services and decisions. Obviously, the controlling party must deliver on what it said it would and, therefore, decisions and policies reflect the party position.

On the other hand, there must be no arrogance of office-holding. There needs to be evidence that local government listens to the public, evidence that goes beyond ritualistic forms. A basic part of this strategy appears to be in the deference shown to school unit or neighbourhood associations. Another part appears to be acceptance of minor modifications in decisions as proposed by coopted members of the education committee. This is also evident in the little things done at the request of school governors, usually through the councillors who hold appointments on these boards. The strategy seems to be to avoid the building up of discontents which could be used by those outside of local government as bases for arousing the electorate. The obverse of the strategy is to have all problems referred back into the committee or the party for disposition.

Finally, it must be concluded that local interest groups do get to participate, to criticize and contribute through the normal controlled points of access to local government. The effect they have is minimal because the controlling party filters and blends their demands through the party ideas of what should be done in education, just as it does with other requests. This is all very fair and it is except that the party position belongs solely to the party. By neutralizing other sources of influence, its power to push through a programme is overwhelming.

The chief education officer

The relationship between the chief education officer and the majority party is crucial to the allocation of resources. On this Jennings comments:

The party comes in with a position or set of aims. The CEO has the task of saying what is good educationally, feasible in the authority, and getting it implemented through the policy

83

process. He is also responsible for telling the majority what won't work. When questions are raised in the community, when interest groups bring in their ideas, the CEO evaluates them for the majority. If the majority wants to adopt or reject such ideas, it does so on the advice of the CEO. However, it is quite clear that the CEO does not advocate nor defend his ideas or those of others on the strength of interest group influence and power.

The chief education officer is a vital servant of the majority political party. At best he can ensure that the party makes sound educational judgements. Distribution of resources must be acceptable or at least defensible to their constituents and to the teachers in the service. In so doing the chief education officer can assist the survival not only of education but also of the party. But his advice is only likely to be acceptable if he is able to present it in a form that is consistent with the party ideology. And he must be equally able to perform a similar role when the majority party changes and a new political ideology prevails. His position is as head of the local education civil service (it is however a position which may take many and occasionally divided forms in the corporate management strategies now being adopted by some of the large British local authorities).

Policy into practice

In this chapter so far we have sighted abundant evidence of the personnel involved in the ecological decision making, their organizational affiliations and their interrelationships. Certainly there has been plenty of evidence of the outcome of their actions. The underlying importance of policy has been unmistakable throughout – the policies of interest groups and individuals and the transcendental policies of the political groups. But how are these policies put into practice by the chief education officer and his staff? The policies formulated may lack detail. They may be both global and fundamental but no more. For example, a decision may be made to redistribute the *allocation* of resources through educational priority type strategies or a decision may be made to redistribute *access* to resources through a policy of comprehensivization.

There may be more detailed policies that resolve questions such as 'should resources be given to areas that already receive them?' which because such a policy is established is likely to receive public acceptability. Alternatively, should the resources be given to new areas of need even at the risk of offending established interest groups? And if new areas of need arc to be given resources, then how is the extent of their need to be assessed? New needs are almost unlimited in education. Every conference contains at least one speaker who is able to define a new need and make a convincing case for it. In the last round of conferences attended by the writer speakers have advocated and won enthusiastic applause for argument for provision of unattached youth counsellors and for education information bureaux in supermarkets. Potential demand is not only unlimited but often it is uncostable and non-assessable. Should the prevailing political party divert more resources to areas where the loudest voices are raised or where their votes are more crucial? It may even be that policies attend to even finer details. Should there be an emphasis on providing resources for the teaching of applied science and technology or on liberal and community studies?

At some stage the political discussion has to stop and the matters left to the professional administrators to be translated into buildings, books, laboratory equipment, teachers' salaries and the long list of other expenditures. How is this to be done?

At the administrators' level much will depend on the internal organization of the education office. The office may take account of the capacities (and incapacities) of individuals recognizing their idiosyncrasies and their strengths. Alternatively, it may be organized on a role oriented, job description regime. In one roles may fit people in an 'organic' manner, in another people may be fitted to roles in a mechanical pattern. If there is a distinction between professional staff (advisers and education officers) and non-professional staff then the political debate may be re-enacted within the education office. In an office the professionals may tend to advocate the redistribution of resources; the non-professional administrators may prefer established paths. In another office the situation may be reversed. The office may be organized around objectives – every new proposal having to be accompanied by a rigorous analysis of the likely consequences – or it may be an office where the responsibilities are delegated and 'officers are given their heads'. Planning may be long term or episodic. It may be by sectors within the office with a range of largely self-contained subdepartments responsible for various areas of resource provision. It may even be intersectorial across local government department boundaries, as in some strategies of corporate management in which decisions on educational resources and county planning may be seen as a combined exercise. An example of this would be an attempt to determine which communities are to be seen as capable of growth in a five year county or city development plan. Here the education officers and the county planning officers may engage in contemporary rather than in sequential discussions.

There is a plethora of management styles available for use with models of rationality, cost development analysis, production flows and a wide range of systems approaches. Most education officers will be familiar with some studies of management, though few will have studied management in spite of the enthusiasm of such bodies as the British Educational Administration Association.

Surrounded by the political atmosphere of the prevailing party, the constraints of central government, the competing currents of demands, the unassessable responses, the bewildering range of management styles, coupled with his own human weaknesses and lack of training, how is the education officer to respond? Mclure (1968) and Byrne (1976) suggest some of the answers in their analyses using sample figures of resource allocation from local education authorities. Using their analyses we can see that in any one year estimates for spending on resources in the local education authority are commonly considered under three broad heads:

1 Expenditure to maintain the existing system as it is. This will usually call for the previous year's pattern of expenditure to be repeated, augmented by what extra is needed to allow for inflation, changes in suppliers and other technical matters.

2 Expenditure to develop the existing system along the lines originally agreed or at least envisaged when it was set up. This new but committed expenditure may also need an inflation addition.

3 A usually small proportion of expenditure for new developments – usually the most vulnerable category.

In addition to these three predictable items, there is commonly:

4 Crisis provision. A range of expenditure on resources that could not have been foreseen but which are inescapable. In any one year these may include such diverse items as: the

collapse of school buildings due to their being built with high alumina cement or some other structural error; an unexpected surge of immigrant population or children electing to stay on after the minimum leaving age; the introduction of new fire regulations which call for the replacement of flammable materials used in schools; the identification of asbestos as a health hazard – all these and many more constitute immediate and inescapable resource provisions.

Defensive reflexes

Such a strategy of resource allocation is widespread because it has many attractions. It makes life more bearable for the administrator because it avoids the need for handling an unpleasantly large number of uncertainties. It makes life more secure for the politician because it minimizes the political risks, and such a strategy can be partly reinforced by what Byrne has called *defensive reflexes*. These are used to absolve the education officers or the politicians for apparent inconsistencies or even errors in the allocation of resources. They also minimize the need for any change in procedure in subsequent years. Byrne quotes a well-known example of the defensive reflex. When challenged by evidence of uneven distribution of examination results between regions, social classes, sexes or even schools, the education officer or politician may reply, 'Success in examinations doesn't necessarily mean that one is educated.' Byrne notes that some of the strongest defensive reflexes are those that respond to monitoring of school attainment by 'external bodies', such as for example the monitoring currently being undertaken by the Department of Education and Science Assessment of Performance Unit. Such monitoring is seen as a particular threat in that it may provide an irrefutable body of evidence that the allocation of resources is wrong or is at least capable of improvement. Again the reflex replies are classic: 'This takes us back to the era of payment by results' is typical.

Yet attractive as the defensive reflexes are to those who use them, and convincing as they may sound when fluently articulated, they are no substitute for a rational administrative policy. Indeed they have no more rationality than the three or four stage planning we have listed here. As Mclure pointed out, such a strategy of 'automatic growth' fails to address itself to the real decisions – should existing deployment of resources be allowed to continue unchallenged? Instead of growth should there be redeployment? Should administrative officers be employed in schools instead of highly expensive teachers working as administrative heads of departments? Should many schools have the sole use of playing fields constructed at considerable expense? Should expensive resources such as laboratories, workshops and libraries be used more intensively even by groups and individuals outside the system? Such alternatives are not always explored; our discussions so far in this chapter have displayed some of the obvious difficulties that would arise if they were. Instead, education officers join with politicians in a global argument for the diversion of *additional* public funds to education, saying 'We need more money to improve the resources of education'. In a real sense this may be the most defensive reflex of all – a defence against the difficult alternative of redeployment.

Our consideration of the role of educational administrators in resource distribution has shown that, like the politicians, their decisions are not infrequently based upon beliefs and ideological positions rather than any set of fundamentally objective procedures. Less explicit and more effectively defended than political groups, they are nonetheless as subjective as the more familiar political ideologies. Once again we end a chapter of this book with the realization of the overriding importance of personal interpretation in the total fabric of education. This is not of course to say that the structure that these interpretations create is subjective and transitory. On the contrary, it is real, firm and enduring and its effect on the lives of participants is substantial and often largely inescapable.

In our discussion of ideology at the conclusion of this book, the administrative arrangements of education will provide not only an appropriate example of the importance of ideology in the determination of ecology but also an effective illumination of the link between ideology and the enduring but not necessarily unchanging structural features of the ecological environment that education constitutes.

Conclusion

In reaching a consideration of the interaction between the majority political party and the chief education officer and his staff and its outcome, we have reached the culmination of our review of the local process of resource distribution. It is a process of allocation that has been described with little mention of such concepts as output measures or accountability. The omissions are unavoidable. It is a process that is determined by a mixture of desired policies, traditional practices, assumptions, expectations and even valiant hopes of response rather than by any general process of evaluation.

This is not to say that links between resources and response do not exist. Unquestionably they do and they may often be causal, as we indicated in the last chapter. Even less is it to say that resource expenditure is not carefully estimated, thoroughly debated, rigorously budgeted and scrupulously supervised. It is, and in times of severe restraint in public expenditure such control will be intensified. But apart from a strictly limited range of evaluation – in a few curriculum projects, for example – fully scientific resource management does not exist. If it is to come at all, then it must await the more optimistic outcomes of bodies such as the Department of Education and Science Assessment of Performance Unit.

But if the process of allocation is obscure in displaying its links between resources and response, it is unambiguously revealing of its links between process and power. In this chapter we have done no less than identify the distribution of educational resources as a legitimate manifestation of power, reviewed the competition to possess it and examined its exercise by those who succeed. But it must be noted that it is a pursuit and exercise of power not only by those who allocate resources but also by those who, by the nature of their response, also exercise important elements of control.

Together the providers and the consumers, not infrequently the same people, determine the ecology of education. We shall talk of the ideologies that guide them in our final chapter. But before that we shall devote a chapter to the micro-ecology of the school where, in somewhat smaller scale, we shall find parallels for the macro-patterns of allocation, response and process that have been considered so far.

Summary

This chapter has reviewed the process of resource allocation, initially at the level of central government but predominantly at local level. The interplay between a wide range of participants has been described and the interaction analysed. The central role of the party system, the importance of its ideology and its relationship with the chief education officer have been identified as crucial areas of the local process of educational resource allocation.

5

Micro-ecology: the school and the classroom as an environment

For most people the dominant feature of the ecology of education is the school. It is a feature that impinges most strongly on their consciousness, involving them inescapably for some of the most formative years of their lives. The experience of it influences much of what happens to them throughout their lives; their perception of education as a whole is crucially determined by it. For the education service too the school is its focal point. It is here that by far the greatest concentration of resources is assembled – it is the core of educational provision to which all education that precedes it is preparatory and all that follows is consequential.

The whole of this book is about the school. Its dominance is so great that it constitutes almost the totality of the educational ecology of the majority of human beings. Only the minority transport themselves to the protected subecologies provided by the universities, polytechnics, colleges and adult education classes. And even for this minority the route is essentially through the school system, responding to the resources that are devoted to its creation and maintenance. For a few, a somewhat greater control over the resources available to them in the school system may be obtained by a purchase of places in independent or private schools; for the majority the realities of the public distribution of resources for schooling constitute the personal reality of their educational environment.

But the schools are not only the central core of the ecology of education; what happens in them also helps to determine that ecology. Inevitably much of the ecology of the school, as we have seen, is decided outside its walls by committees and associations of a variety of individuals who have a view about the appropriate nature of schools in the social conditions in which they exist. But power, manifest or latent, also rests within the school. The ways in which the school uses its resources, makes them available to or withholds them from the students and the strategies by which it influences the future availability of resources are as important as any of the processes we have considered so far. In this chapter we shall examine them in greater detail.

How the school distributes its resources

Sometimes schools feel powerless to control their input of resources. Teachers may feel that 'the new school may never be built', that there are perennial shortages of books, stationery, laboratory equipment and all other necessary material resources. Requests for alleviation may appear to sink without trace into the bureaucracy of the local education office. Yet, in practice, all schools enjoy substantial discretion in the allocation of a substantial supply of resources to different categories of students. There are many decisions that have to be taken within the school – selecting examination classes, the distribution of teaching roles, the distribution of access to laboratories, workshops and other specialist facilities.

Schools vary in the extent to which they may exercise discretion in varying the categories of resources they receive. Almost all have some choice in deciding which books they shall receive from funds earmarked for book purchase, which laboratory equipment they shall receive from their equipment allocation. Other schools may have the discretion to buy more or fewer books in a system of *virement* wherein money can be switched from books to science equipment or games equipment and vice versa. The extent of *virement* varies between local authorities but most limit this by specifying 'minimum standards of equipment' in various areas of the school. Much rarer is the possibility of *virement* between materials and staff salaries, though Briault (1974) does indicate a prospect of *virement* between teaching and non-teaching staff:

> Schools and colleges differ very widely in the curriculum they provide and in the ways in which they set about the task of providing learning opportunities for their pupils or their students. In some schools there may be a readiness to use non-personal learning resources of wide variety; in others there may be an unwillingness to do so. There should, therefore, be the opportunity within the school to consider, not only how it should expend its capitation in terms of materials and equipment, but also to consider that expenditure in relation to the expenditure on non-teaching staff and on teachers. For example, each school should have to consider extensions of its curriculum or the provision of very small teaching groups against the demand that such arrangements make, not simply on teaching staff, but on total resources. The school would then be in a position to recognize and to take decisions about its needs on the one hand for more teachers to provide greater variety in the curriculum (to staff new 'A' level subjects for example), and its desire on the other hand to improve its clerical and librarian support in the library or its technician support in the science field or the field of educational technology.

Yet even here Briault goes on to indicate the constraints that must surround such *virement*:

> The transfer of these powers of choice, and hence of management responsibility, to the individual school or college need not conflict with the final overall responsibility of the education authority for the maintenance of standards. The Authority can, and should, arrange important safeguards. For example, an Authority can lay down a basic minimum teaching staff for all its establishments, and in the school field this may well bear a direct relationship to the quota, as long as that continues. It may wish to lay down minimum standards of office and support staff, nursery assistants in nursery schools and classes, perhaps of technician assistants in laboratories and the like. These too must be regarded as basic staff who must be employed, and of course the Authority has an obligation for continuing employment to those whom it has put on its permanent staff, whether teachers or non-teaching staff.

Within the school, however, there are likely to be areas of decision making that go far beyond the availability of *virement*. Heads of department in secondary schools exercise substantial discretion over the collection and distribution of departmental resources. The specialized and rapidly changing nature of many subject areas may ensure that they are largely free from detailed oversight by the head who is unlikely to be able to remain in close touch with new developments in all areas of the curriculum (in many local education authorities there is, however, some oversight by specialist subject advisers).

But of even greater importance is the belief in *professional autonomy* which is now being espoused by many individual classroom teachers. It is a view which sees the teacher in control of the situation in the classroom. It is he who decides what is taking place and his decisions are a consequence of his professional judgement. He may exercise it in terms of his understanding of child development, his understanding of the needs of individual pupils or even his grasp of the fundamental nature of knowledge itself and the way it should be presented and made available to different categories of students. Acting in these ways his professional judgement is backed by his professional and academic training. This model of professional 'sovereignty' is seen to be to some extent modified by a few external constraints, but even these may be of diminishing significance. The examination system appears to be being brought under the control of teachers through Mode 3 strategies and teacher-dominated advisory panels. HMI and local Inspectors become translated to Advisers, while the introduction of more democratic patterns of school management tend to diminish the overriding power of the head. Curriculum development, with its emphasis on diversity, spontaneity and the ensuing choice by the individual teacher from a wide range of options, in any case makes it difficult for the head, or even the head of a department to oversee the work of the teacher in the detailed way that was possible when the curricular options open to him were both more restricted and more predictable.

Whilst the view of teacher autonomy unquestionably exceeds reality in many schools, it is in its existence of far greater importance than the actual consequences in the day to day life of the classroom. It represents a new dimension in the dynamics of power in the school, articulating a claim by the classroom teacher for a larger and more effective voice in the allocation of resources in the school for materials and for non-teaching assistants to enable him to do the things that as a professional teacher he believes are necessary for the children he teaches.

Yet although the claim for voice in the distribution of resources may appear to be individualized and even spontaneous it is not difficult to pick out a pattern of ideological positions which are adopted by many teachers. These are global positions which, like the political party ideologies that we have seen in our consideration of the local authorities, are general rather than specific, continuing rather than episodic.

Two main ideologies may be identified, broadly labelled traditional and progressive. Vaughan and Archer (1971) have emphasized the long term nature of ideologies of these kinds; what is of more recent date is their institutionalization and reification. Traditional orientations to an allocation of resources suitable for established forms of school organization, curriculum and teaching methods had seldom needed an articulated written defence until the development of a well documented progressive/radical alternative orientation. Such a stage occurred in the 1960s and it was at about this time that the various movements for the maintenance of traditional standards came into existence and adopted written as well as spoken forms of advocacy. Notable British examples were the *Black Papers* and the Campaign for Educational Standards. Eggleston (1973) has set out a detailed comparison of the two ideological positions and their use in the schools. On the one hand there is the traditional orientation which emphasizes commitment to long established forms of learning, standards, institutions and value systems. The progressive orientation on the other hand espouses new understandings, new socially relevant studies, multi-purpose flexible institutions, contractual relationships and a more open distribution of knowledge – essentially a view of resource allocation and response that emphasizes the personal perspective of teachers. Though both orientations are widespread, often occurring within the same school, analysis suggests that there are clear indications of a gradual but unmistakable move from the traditional to the progressive ideology with unmistakable consequences for the allocation of resources. It is a view of the school, its resources and its power structure, that has close connections with the Durkheimian concept of symbolic order rather than with the Weberian concept of structure, as Bernstein (1971) has pointed out.

Resources and social control

Although the distribution of resources in school reflects both the ideologies and the power structure that exist in the school, the manner in which it is undertaken has central implications for the distribution of power in society. The availability or non-availability of teaching or other resources to a student can critically determine his own opportunities to exercise power as an adult. The selection, identification and distribution of those to whom such opportunities are given by the schools will, to a large measure, decide the social structure and the distribution of power in the future society. It is argued by writers such as Bowles and Gintis (1977) that the major objective in the allocation of resources in the schools within the education system is to ensure the continuation of the existing social system by distributing and using resources in such a way as to create the 'right numbers' of people holding 'the right skills and values' for the needs of the economic system. In short the task of the schools is seen to be to preserve the social ecology intact by acting as instruments of social control.

There is some evidence that suggests that the distribution of resources may be along such lines. Lacey in his study of *Hightown Grammar* (1970) showed that in that school the heads of departments exercised the key roles in the allocation of resources to the students, including the allocation of teachers. Lacey reported that the most senior and experienced teachers tended to be allocated to the upper streams and examination classes. Conversely, 65 per cent of the first and second year teaching and 85 per cent of the bottom stream teaching was done by non-senior or inexperienced teachers. He draws attention to the circular nature of the situation – teachers working with low status classes were usually seen to lack professional standing, and this in turn diminished their capacity to successfully claim materials and equipment for their classes. Such arrangements not only cause a major unevenness in the distribution of resources to different categories of pupil but also leave unanswered more searching questions regarding the appropriate amount of resources each pupil needs or it entitled to.

The incidence of social control may take a less physical form; it may even occur in the classroom of a teacher with a strong commitment to egalitarian reform and social redistribution.

A good example of these difficulties was to be seen in the

work of a young teacher in his classroom which the writer was able to see when he undertook a number of periods of observation with his students. The teacher was working in an English primary school, noted for progressive and individualized methods with children ranging from seven through to eleven years of age. The teacher was conducting a project on medical services. For several sessions the classroom became a hospital. The pupils played the roles of doctors, nurses and other hospital personnel. Quite clearly many children were learning not only about anatomy and first aid but also about the diagnosis and decision making central to the work of a hospital service. Yet the writer developed a feeling of unease after this apparently successful project had continued for a number of sessions. Whilst many of the children appeared to be gaining much from the work, a number of others appeared to gain much less.

On inspection children appeared to be divided into three groups. The first was a small group of fluent, confident and generally well spoken children who tended to take the key roles in the project. These children formed the nucleus from which the consultants, matrons, anaesthetists and other key decision makers were regularly drawn. The second rather larger group consisted of children who performed such tasks as nursing assistants, hospital orderlies, porters and a multitude of other 'walk on' parts involving relatively little speech and a minimum of decision making. Most experienced a substantial amount of standing and waiting. The third category not immediately visible were the pool of accident victims. These children spend substantial parts of the sessions on stretchers and swathed in bandages. On occasions these bandages covered not only the limbs but often the face, making speech and even sight and hearing difficult. Not only were these three groups clearly divided in all project activities but also for most part their composition was similar. In many ways this progressive classroom with its strong emphasis on egalitarianism and child-centred approaches showed a remarkable resemblance to the streamed educational arrangements that had preceded it. Though for the teacher all children were 'benefiting' from the rich resources available in this outstandingly well equipped school, some children were unquestionably benefiting more than others. Moreover, the distribution seemed to have a very considerable element of 'social reproduction' built into it.

There are many other examples to be seen in the schools. Ford (1968), in her study of comprehensive schools, showed how in a situation of open access to resources, different categories of children secured a greater share than others. In particular, middle class children seemed to be far more effective at gaining access to the out of school facilities for clubs, sports, drama, hobbies and the like – facilities that in the comprehensive schools under review were often abundantly equipped with appropriate materials and equipment. The process of self-regulated use of resources is often reinforced by the system of cooling out, whereby students come to see themselves as unable or unenthusiastic to follow courses taught by highly qualified, specialist teachers using extensive library and laboratory resources. Instead such pupils 'select' lower status courses. These courses may not necessarily be lower cost ones – metalwork, woodwork and home economics in particular may involve higher material resource cost per student than most other subjects. Yet they are seldom more expensive in their demands on the most costly school resource – that of teachers' salaries.

One of the most developed analyses of social control in the primary school is that of Sharp and Green (1975). The writers show how children may be ascribed identities that appear to make them unsuitable for access to certain kinds of resource in the school. Such a child is Michael:

> Nothing I said would make any difference, you know, he wouldn't ... he didn't want to write or anything, he wasn't very interested in that. He wasn't very interested in joining in with a reading group – he wasn't very interested in the story. He just wanted to go on his own sweet way ... he just dribbed and drabbed about ... you know, he never had a true friend. But he's ever so willing to join in if you organize a little group – and he'll join in and he'll be, you know, quite an important member of that group – but he doesn't *need* to ... I can't make up my mind why he is so peculiar.

Speaking about such children in general one of the teachers at the school under review, 'Mapledene', says:

> In an ideal situation you'd have them all so keen and interested that they'd get on and just come to you for book references and this and that and the other [laughter] but here they don't seem to get involved in anything, not for any length of time anyway. They've got a very short span of concentration, they've got no perseverance at all. You've got to be standing over them, all the time, pushing them.

The writers explore in detail the circumstances which lead the teachers to differentiate between children and their resources in this way and to become, despite their evident concern for children, 'agents' of social control. Sharp and Green suggest that this arises from a series of societal expectations that surround the schools and teachers and which are internalized into the personal ideologies of the teachers through the long process of personal and professional socialization – such a socialization process inhibits or at least fails to encourage the development of coherent and workable alternative ideologies.

One of the most striking illustrations of the use of resources in the schools is that offered by Wax and Wax (1964) in their account of Indian reservation schoolchildren in North America, an account confirmed by visits of the writer to Canadian reservation schools. They offer a cautionary tale with which to match more superficial analogies of school enrichment strategies. The reservation schools visited by Wax and Wax were abundantly supplied with resources including well qualified teachers and impressive equipment. This favourable allocation arose from a policy of enrichment that attempted to compensate for the deficient educational ecology of the reservations.

On visiting the schools, the researchers found that impressive facilities not only existed but were indeed being put to use. Yet teachers complained that the response of the Indian children was still disappointing, implying in confidence that the whole exercise was a waste of money. The researchers watched several lessons given by white American teachers. One in particular was a lesson on water, dealing with the plumbing systems of a modern American home complete with hot and cold water, drainage and heating systems. The response of the Indian students was minimal despite the impressive efforts of the teacher in presenting his subject with a wide range of teaching aids. The teacher, after the lesson, indicated that this response was, alas, typical. Yet the researchers, found that although the understanding of water as used by the white Americans was only faintly grasped by the children they nevertheless had very clear concepts of water that were relevant to their own culture. They were able to speak enthusiastically of mountain streams, fishing, finding water in drought and many other aspects of the theme that had been entirely missing from the lesson they experienced. It is suggested that what is happening in such a situation may be a use of resources by the school in a manner that intensifies feelings of inferiority and even failure on the part of children by demonstrating to them their inadequate knowledge of the 'dominant culture' and the inferiority of their own culture. It may also lead them to accept that the only way that they are likely to be able to obtain high status in American society is to forsake their own culture and begin the long and difficult internalization of white American culture. Interpretations such as this have led to considerable new debate on the educational resources for Indian schools in both the United States and Canada and attempts to find ways of revaluating the relationship between Indian and white cultures.

Schools and resource take-up

So far our argument has been based on the assumption that, regardless of its ideological orientations, the school distributes its resources fully, and none are wasted. This is not a valid assumption; many local education officers can 'in confidence' name schools where spending on books, materials and equipment is substantially below maximum permitted levels. Heads of schools will speak of wasteful and unnecessary expenditure ceilings. Once again, we are reminded that there is virtually no established attempt to quantify precisely the resources needed by any child for any specific activity. And inevitably there are many inherent areas of 'waste' in any school. An incoming head of department may view the school's existing stock of textbooks in his subject with disdain and insist on their replacement. His reasons for doing so may in part be academic; they may also be in part an attempt to establish the mark of his new regime. New examination regulations or even new editions of texts may lead to the same consequences. The shelves of no longer used textbooks in many school store cupboards testify to the frequency of such changes.

It may also happen that the school rejects or fails to use its resources for other reasons. One of the notable problem areas seems to be connected with major curriculum development projects. Shipman, Bolam and Jenkins (1974), in their study of the Keele Integrated Studies Project, show how, in a number of the trial schools, the extent of resources provided by the project were unused, incompletely used or even misused. The visits to schools suggest that such a state of affairs is in no way uncommon.

A characteristic of curriculum development is the decline of

100

school commitment to a project. Enthusiasm for an innovation is likely to be greatest at the outset. The prospects of a new and 'free' supply of ideas and even resources for the work of the classroom are attractive especially if the project promises to focus resources on some of the more difficult areas of the curriculum where the school is experiencing problems. There is always the prospect that this project will be 'the project', participation in which will bring fame and renown to the school and its teachers.

But as time passes the situation is likely to change. There will inevitably be some problems, possibly many, in the use and adaptation of the project materials to the work of the school. Some successful existing curriculum practices may be challenged and even have to be abandoned if the project is to be taken fully. Timetable changes and other organizational disruptions may be necessary. Key members of staff who are most heavily involved in the project may move to different appointments; this happened frequently in some of the Keele Project schools. In some cases the teacher's very involvement in the project is likely to be the factor in his upward professional mobility. The replacement members of staff may be less interested in the project and certainly will have lacked the initial impetus of the early stages in the school.

Faced with the inevitable difficulties, deprived of the initial leadership in the school and unwilling to abandon successful longstanding practices, marginal staff tend to become more marginal, even disaffected. At the end of the day the usage of many project resources seems to be fragmentary. Some teachers will use a substantial part of the resources provided of the project; most will have adopted bits and pieces and used them to modify, to a greater or lesser extent, their existing resources. Packages will have been taken apart, some of the contents adopted and others discarded. The result will be a *mélange* composed of items from various projects, a range of opinions on how it may be used, further material generated within the school from time to time, the whole gradually modifying the teacher's stock of resources in a highly pragmatic and often unplanned way.

Schools and the creation of resources

The distribution of resources and their acceptance or rejection by the school is of fundamental importance. But the school may also have an active as well as a passive role in relation to its resources. A number of strategies exist whereby the school creates new demands for resources that local authorities and even the central government may find it difficult not to respond to. A determined school staff can ensure suitable media treatment of the shortcomings of its resources, whether of laboratories or lavatories, that cannot be ignored. In its campaign it may well be supported by professional bodies, parent–teacher associations and local branches of national pressure groups. In times of economic difficulty it may be that successful strategies of this kind provide one of the few certain ways to ensure major advantages in new buildings or special allowances over and above basic 'system maintenance' allocations.

Campaigns do not exhaust the strategies open to schools. An effective way of ensuring new equipment lies within the examination system. If the school is instrumental in introducing a new 'Mode 3' examination syllabus for its students (that is, a syllabus specific to itself) that is subsequently endorsed by the Examination Board, then the local education authority is faced with a *fait accompli*. The necessary materials and equipment to sustain the courses for all the students who follow it are almost certain to be found.

Schools may also be instrumental in introducing new curricula that are endorsed by strong specialist interests such as a local or even a national curriculum development body or even a powerful local employer (a detailed account of some of the ways in which a curriculum project may be established through a school initiative is presented by Eggleston, 1977). Whatever strategy is used, professional or public legitimation of the activity constitutes an important addition to the power of the school to seek official resources to sustain and develop.

Sometimes such initiative may take a very localized form. One example known to the writer occurred in a secondary school serving a large inter-war housing estate. The estate was neglected; the adolescent population had a reputation for vandalism and near delinquency. A small group of newly appointed teachers initiated a Community Service Project wherein the teachers, with the senior pupils, conducted an impressive programme of socially approved activity whereby the boys and girls dug old peoples' gardens, painted their walls, cleared the local brook of debris and generally brought acceptable material improvements to a somewhat deprived housing estate. There was widespread local approval for the project and the pupils were praised by the mayor and the local newspaper. There was local relief that the school through its project had 'transformed' the pupils. The local authority voted extra earmarked resources to the school to further the project.

The next phase of the project was based on a realization that the old people had greater problems than weedy gardens. They had difficulty in obtaining their rate rebates, the local council was tardy in the repair of roofs and other maintenance of a kind that was beyond the scope of the pupils. With the teacher the pupils decided that some further action was needed and wrote to the local newspaper and to the local housing committee about the problems, urging immediate action. The response was quite different in nature from that which they had enjoyed previously. This time the local paper was distinctly unenthusiastic about their 'interference', defining the pupils as 'young troublemakers' and the teachers as 'politically motivated'. The coincidence that the chairman of the Local Housing Committee was also a member of the Local Education Committee appeared to lead to several problems within the school. Certainly the teacher was encouraged not to continue with this particular line of action and the additional resources ceased to be available.

In this 'case study' there is a very obvious and familiar example of the capacity of the school to obtain additional resources – either through the local education authority or even from the community at large. And there is also a very clear indication of the way in which the overall process of social control can be imposed upon the work of the school if the school does not appear to be exercising social control through its own initiatives. In this case there was widespread local approval of the adolescents when they appeared to be 'fitting in' more closely to the social system than they had before. This was followed by widespread anxiety when the school appeared to be leading them to participate, however marginally, in local decision making – to exercise some 'power' in the community. Such an initiative by schools opens up the prospect, however minimally, of a redistribution of power in a community, reducing some of the power of those at present exercising it and transferring it to a previously powerless and allegedly 'irresponsible' group. In the example the power sought was in part that which was held by those who also influenced the distribution of educational resources and the response was predictable. Yet the termination of the project did not mean that it was a failure. The students made visible gains in their capacity to formulate a case, to articulate it effectively and to express it confidently. Several of the students are now playing a part in the power structure of local union branches and one is under consideration for candidature for local government election.

The perception of school resources

We have emphasized the importance of the ways in which resources are perceived on many occasions in this book. The ways in which they are interpreted by individuals crucially affect their response to what is provided. The ecology of the school is no exception – it is a different ecology for different individuals. In particular, the perceptions of the children are likely to be fundamentally different from those of the teachers.

On first entering school, the child is likely to be concerned with the spatial aspects of his environment, feeling out the territory available to him in the classroom and in the playground and, particularly, identifying his personal space and its resources – the desks and chairs, the books and pencils, the clothes hooks and aprons. In schools where resources are not compartmentalized and the emphasis is on sharing, it may be that the child has great difficulty in identifying his personal environment. Much the same seems to occur when teachers find that they have to share their resources – for example, the resources of the day school being also the resources of the evening programme of the community college. Characteristically attempts at compartmentalization begin with the locked 'evening institute cupboard' standing alongside the locked 'school cupboard', keys being available only to the 'rightful' users. In this way 'they' are prevented from 'abusing' or even wrecking 'our' resources.

Children and teachers often seek what Steele (1973) has labelled *privacy*:

> When people complain of not having enough privacy they are usually saying that they have no way of controlling their relation to their social surroundings because: (*a*) they cannot control who comes into contact with them and when; (*b*) they cannot prevent their conversations from being overheard; or (*c*) they cannot prevent being observed by others.

The concept of privacy is clearly relevant to much of the use that is made of resources in the school. Often the concept itself is indicated in physical form by built boundaries or painted lines.

More often, however, the boundaries are invisible yet nonetheless clearly recognized and unquestionably effective. Gould (1976) writes:

> In an Edwardian primary school where the writer once worked several classrooms were connected directly together. A group of three rooms had been built as a single block. The entrance to the first was through a cloakroom, the second was entered through the first and the third through the second. So the middle classroom acted as a passageway between the others. It was accepted by the teacher in the middle room that other staff and pupils would come through her room at break times and at change of lessons and in addition children with special messages from members of staff, teachers and visitors would frequently pass through.
>
> Bad as this might sound, both from the point of view of interruptions of lessons and that of group privacy there came to exist a tolerable *modus vivendi*. A right of way was tacitly accepted which followed round the wall of the middle classroom and which became 'corporate space'. People who used it made a perfunctory tap on the door, nodding to the teacher in the middle room, and generally they were ignored by most of the occupants, provided they kept to within the bounds of the right of way. When, very occasionally, either teachers or pupils took a route through the main body of the room which violated the boundary it was regarded as an intrusion and all activity stopped until the intruder had left.

Though there is a growing literature on the relationship between architecture, furnishing and personal behaviour, there has been remarkably little study of the way in which the building, location of equipment, wall covering and other features of the physical environment affect the behaviour of those in schools. Many assumptions have been and are made. Early school builders believed that the school should not detract children from learning and provided plain walls and high windows to ensure this. Contemporary architects believe with equal fervour that school buildings should stimulate children and use brightly painted walls and low windows whilst teachers who work in them fill the rooms with the visual stimulation. In such areas of resource provision, as in many others, we have little hard knowledge of the consequences of predictable disputes between 'arbitrary authoritarian school architects' and 'unadventurous blinkered teachers' who compete for power in such contested areas of resources provision. It is highly probable that the capacity of the school to organize the physical setting of its resources in order to maximize its efficiency is still far short of what is possible.

Some of the potential of this area of study has been glimpsed by Richardson in her book *The Environment of Learning* (1967). She writes of the important differences in learning that seem to arise from rearranging the chairs or the other props in the classroom. She also writes of the perception of resources that can sometimes lead to a higher evaluation of old and time-expired than of new and expensive ones:

> In these days of fairly rapid building programmes, it not infrequently happens that a whole school has to move from an old building to a new one. Such a school may be an object of envy to neighbouring schools that see no prospect of escape from shabby old premises. Yet to the staff and children who are involved in such a move, the experience is unlikely to be wholly pleasant. A visitor may expect to find, in the new building, a mood of elation. What he may find, however, is a mood of depression and disappointment, accompanied by a good deal of nostalgia for the (now) loved old building. Complaints about the new one may be legion. The position of the headmaster's room and the office, the narrowness of the staircase, the inadequacy of the locker space, the mistakes in the design of the apparently splendid stage – all these may excite loud comment. Little or nothing may be said about the lightness and airiness of the classrooms, the extended laboratory and gymnasium accommodation, the pleasant views from the windows, the more spacious and attractive hall. And there may even be some envy of the school that has now taken over the old building.

A striking example of the transformations of a new building back into 'old' form was seen by the writer on a visit to a large new secondary school. Provision had been made for a large open plan integrated craft and design area. One of the first 'projects' undertaken by the art, woodwork, metalwork and technical drawing specialists using the building was to build walls with hardboard and slotted steel angles that effectively divided the area into the specialist rooms they had occupied in the previous school building.

Unquestionably an important feature of the individual response

106

to the environment of the school is the personal feeling of identity. It may well be that the individual can only use ecological environment in the school and elsewhere if he can make it part of himself by actively relating with it. Nicholson (1972) has gone so far as to suggest in his 'theory of loose parts' that the more successfully designers create a 'no-participant environment' the more successfully will people attempt to participate and establish their individual presence in it, even to the extent of behaviour which is labelled as vandalism. The 'structural modifications' that take place in waiting rooms and public conveniences help to make Nicholson's point, as do the adornments on the books and the carvings on desks in the classroom. It may well be that in our consideration of the provision of the components of the education environment we pay too much attention to their technical qualities and insufficient attention to their personal qualities. There is little doubt that we largely fail to consider the powerful need felt by the individual to personalize his environment – to create a specific and often private ecology rather than a shared one.

Resources and student choice

But the perception of the school's resources is not restricted to their physical properties. Students, teachers, parents and employers characteristically hold perception about the nature of school subjects – their usefulness or uselessness, the pleasure or the boredom to which they give rise, their feelings and their relationships towards them. The Schools Council report *Young School Leavers* (1968) shows how strikingly varied such views can be and also how firmly held they commonly are. As the school system takes on a more open and flexible form such views are likely to have increasing consequences for the distribution of resources in schools. In many comprehensive schools and in the greater part of post-school education course enrolments are predominantly determined by student preference. Though the comprehensive school may provide a wide range of courses for its fourth and fifth year students, if the option course is genuine then some courses are likely to be heavily subscribed and others lightly subscribed with important consequences not only for the demand for materials and equipment but also for the demand for specialist staffing. Neave (1975) has shown how response to student demand has radically changed the range of course provision in many comprehensive schools in England and Wales, creating a situation totally different from that of the recent past when heads and senior staff of schools were able to evolve a long term pattern of course provision secure in the knowledge that they would be able to allocate the 'correct' type and numbers of students to them. It was an era in which the length of school life could be effectively predicted at eleven-plus – those passing the selection examination would almost certainly stay on; those who did not would almost certainly leave at the minimum leaving age. Taylor (1963), in his account of the development of the secondary modern school, charted the persistent efforts of a small band of schools to make resources for extended education available to all who could and wished to use them rather than only to those who had passed the eleven-plus – to help all to 'contract in' to the competitive world of social and educational advancement from which many had been excluded at the eleven-plus. As a consequence of such efforts and the more general changes in the social evaluation of education, students' decisions to 'stay on' are now characteristically made at any time up to minimum leaving age and are, in large measure, made in the light of experience of the resources of the school, particularly the teaching resources, and the personal interpretation of their consequences.

A relatively new feature of the British schools system is the introduction of the school counsellor who may also come to play an important part in the determination of the ecology of schooling. In the fullest definition of his role it would be the task of the counsellor to interview, say, all the fourth year students of the school in which he is working, diagnosing their interests, motivations, aptitudes, skills and aspirations. He would also explore the resources of the school system, the occupational opportunities provided locally and nationally and try to identify in the light of his information the appropriate next steps in the careers of the students.

It is possible to imagine the situation in which the counsellor, having surveyed the students and the educational and occupational opportunities in the area, has diagnosed a keen demand for a one year school leavers course in special subjects in the school in the immediate future. His recommendation to the head will therefore be for the replacement of the retiring classics teacher with a new appointment, that of a teacher of typing and commercial subjects and for a substantial part of the equipment fund to be switched to the purchase of typewriters and other office machines. But it may also be that the head is a classics specialist, keen to maintain a longstanding classics tradition in the school and wishing to reappoint a classics specialist to his staff for this purpose. He may also wish to use a substantial part of the available money to purchase the new Cambridge Latin texts to assist the revival of classics teaching of the school. The competition is, for British schools, a novel one, and at the present time it is uncertain which way the decision would go. Even though in a real sense the counsellor has 'mobilized' the power of the students, much is likely to depend on the relative personal standing of the head and the counsellor in the power system within the school.

Cicourel and Kitsuse (1963) suggest, however, that the situation may be by no means as self-evident as this example would suggest. They outline a latent role for the counsellor – not as a diagnostic expert but as a persuader – a member of the school establishment who in his discussions with the students convinces them that the resources the school is prepared to offer them are in fact the resources that are best suited for their needs so the students come to choose precisely the distribution of resources that has been laid down as desirable by the head and the school staff. Yet even if Cicourel and Kitsuse's diagnosis is true it certainly confirms that, however manipulated, no distribution of resources in the schools is likely to be viable unless it takes account of the importance of the perspectives of the students as well as the staff. And there is certainly considerable evidence that the perceptions of clients are, once established, a powerful and enduring element in decision making. As the Royal Statistical Society project on factors influencing the choice of higher education made clear, decisions by students once made were almost wholly impervious to changes in the situation – even changes in university entrance requirements which radically altered the effective range of choice available to the students (Barnard, McCreath and Freeman, 1967).

Conclusion

The ecology of the school and the creation, distribution and use of resources that determines it is clearly a partnership between all who live and work within it. It is an organic, dynamic environment determined by the multitude of perceptions and interactions of individuals. Yet though characterized by flexibility and at times a remarkably fine balance of forces, the ecology of the school has a remarkable degree of permanence and stability, an underlying form that enables it through many apparently fundamental yet in the long run superficial changes, to continue to take the key role in reproducing the social system from generation to generation. There is no evidence that individuals seek through their perceptions, their interpretations or their intentions to challenge the ecological system of schooling or of the society of which it is part. Most seem to seek a more active part in the present system rather than in some alternative system – a conclusion that has also been reached after an extensive research in an examination of informal education in England and Wales through the Youth Service (Eggleston, 1976). It is in the creation and maintenance of this dynamic equilibrium of the schools that the resources of education play their most crucial and inescapable role.

Summary

In this chapter we have considered the ecology of the school by examining the creation and distribution of the resources that constitute it. The evidence for regarding the ecology of the school as an environment of social control is presented and examined in the light of the interpretation and resources of teachers and students.

6

Conclusion: ecology and idealogy

In this volume we have developed an ecological approach to the study of schooling. It is an approach which has endeavoured to transcend systems analyses with their emphases on structure and disciplinary studies which view the school from a limited range of theoretical perspectives. It may be argued that human ecology even transcends interdisciplinarity because it focuses on the total habitat of the human being.

Three major themes

Our exploration over the previous five chapters has identified three major themes that have confirmed abundantly the relevance of an ecological approach to education. The first of these has been the striking evidence of the unevenness of the ecological environment of education – an unevenness that in parts is mountainous rather than merely undulating. It is an unevenness that has been seen within a national system of education, between and within local education authority systems and between and within individual schools. A remarkably similar distribution of unevenness was also to be seen in our analysis of the response to educational provision.

The second major theme that has run through the volume has

been the complex pattern of interrelated factors that contribute to the creation, maintenance, repair and reproduction of the educational ecosystem. Our study has displayed considerable evidence of the relevance of the 'biological' ecological analysis. In particular, the educational system is characterized by its capacity to resist disturbance and by its ability to adapt to unavoidable change with the minimum of disturbance. The defensive strategies that we considered in Chapter 4 provided particularly interesting examples of this tendency for 'system maintenance', but throughout the volume there have been many other examples of the ways in which all participants in the educational process can display a vigorous capacity to preserve their ecological environment intact. It is in the pursuit of this end that much of the power in the system is applied.

The third major theme (perhaps the dominant one) has been the prevailing importance of individual perceptions of the ecological environment and the ways in which these perceptions lead to patterns of decision and action in the creation, use and response to the environment of education. Indeed it is not too great an exaggeration to say that the ecological environment of education is not one but many environments. Certainly it is different for different categories of participants – children, parents, teachers, administrators, elected politicians. But it is also arguably different even for individuals within these categories; each individual participant brings not only his own perception but also his own interpretation to the educational scene. Certainly our examination of the perceptions of provision, the personal nature of response, the various interpretations of politicians and the ways in which these interpretations are themselves perceived by chief education officers and their staff make it clear that we cannot ignore an interpretative framework in our attempt to analyse the nature of the ecology of education.

In this connection Schutz's essay 'Choosing among projects of action' (1967) is of some assistance:

> Our analysis, which we have intentionally restricted to the daily life situation of choosing between projects, started from the world taken for granted beyond question as the general field of our open possibilities. Our biographically determined situation selects certain elements of this field as relevant for our purpose at hand. If this selection meets no obstacle the project is simply transformed into a purpose and the action is carried

112

out as a matter of course. If, by the very vagueness of our knowledge at hand at the time of projecting, a situation of doubt arises, then some of the formerly open possibilities become questionable, problematic. Some part of the world formerly taken for granted beyond question and therefore unquestioned has now been put into question. The decision retransforms what has been made questionable into a certainty, but an empirical certainty that is again an unquestioned element of our knowledge, taken for granted until further notice.

The search for explanation

Certainly if we seek to explain the nature of the ecology of education, Schutz offers us a more promising guide to the nature of decision making and the location of power than does the map of distribution and the attractive but somewhat suspect correlations that it contains. Though there are many instances where the nature of the correlations points to a real likelihood of a causal connection there is in all cases at least an ambiguity that alerts one to the risk that one may after all be looking at no more than two dependent variables.

Though the interpretative approach suggests a more fundamental guide to explanation, it has its own hazard – that of its fragmentary nature. Fortunately, however, in the educational system many of the individual interpretations and the actions that spring from them are assembled by the participants into shared and proclaimed beliefs or ideologies. We have seen many of these collectivities in our analyses – the pressure groups and interest groups, the various specialist and general professional groups, and above all the political parties at central and local level. All these are groups that have not only agreed to adopt shared perceptions and interpretations, but also, in the interests of gaining and maintaining power, have been obliged to declare themselves publicly.

These groups are unlike anything in 'biological' ecology in that they seek to make a positive and concerted change in their ecology. Often, the attempt is made to make change of a dramatic kind – most notably in the compensatory programmes and other interventionist strategies.

The consequences of ecology

Despite the proclaimed intention and unquestionable achievement and exercise of power, there is little evidence that significant change in the educational ecosystem occurs as a result. On the contrary, the outcome of the various groups and their exercise of power seems to be largely to preserve the system in a way that, strikingly, confirms the relevance of the concepts of biological ecology to human ecology. Our examination has shown that the uneven distribution of resources is positively reinforced by central government expenditure constraints, local political considerations and the defensive strategies of the participants. The uneven response is maintained by the remarkable capacity of both teachers and students to respond in longstanding ways even though faced with apparent changes in the distribution of resources. Teachers often teach and students often respond in the comprehensive schools in much the same way as they did in the selective secondary schools that preceded them. Even when faced with challenging new school buildings both teachers and students make concerted efforts to preserve the life style they adopted in the old buildings and even to modify the architecture to facilitate this. And as Lowe and Worboys (1975) have noticed, the study of ecology itself may be transformed for use as a powerful, ideological argument for conservative strategies.

Overall our analysis has suggested that the ecology of schooling changes but slowly if at all. Supported by a wide range of other studies the evidence suggests that the system as a whole, its local manifestations and its individual schools are remarkably stable. Though surface forms change – new schools are built, new teachers appointed and new equipment installed – the fundamental distribution of resources, of response and of opportunity seems to remain substantially unchanged, reflecting the social and economic structure of society rather than the needs and talents of its members.

Sociologists have labelled the system as one characterized by social control or social reproduction. The evidence of this volume fits well with the analyses of writers such as Sharp and Green (1975) and Bowles and Gintis (1977). Is then the ecology of the school part of a greater self-perpetuating ecosystem that, despite the vigorous attempts of some of the inhabitants to intervene, is unmoving and permanent?

In part, the answer is yes. But the analysis has suggested

114

repeatedly that this arises from individual perceptions and interpretations rather than from societal reasons. The pressures to retain the ecosystem as it is seem to spring inexorably from the teachers, students, administrators and parents – who see their roles thrown into uncertainty, their professional capital devalued and their prospects diminished if substantial change is threatened. It may be that such interpretations are the result of some process of social conditioning that affects men, some characteristic of human socialization that gives rise to a 'false consciousness' in his thinking. Or it may spring from alienation that is brought about and even reinforced by the characteristics of the social and economic system. Many writers have explored man's predicament and his prospect of escaping from the human dilemma.

The evidence assembled in this book confirms that man's escape from his ecological environment is encompassed by a series of 'ifs'. Even if his escape is desired it is unlikely to occur through modifications to the ecology of education. Even if such modifications were achievable, substantial differences in the distribution of educational resources would be unlikely. Even if substantial differences in the distribution of educational resources were to occur, it is unlikely that these would produce striking changes in the distribution of educational attainment. Even if striking changes in educational attainment were to occur, there is no clear evidence that significant changes in opportunity would spring from them.

The 'ifs' arise and remain because the environment of education is but one aspect of the total ecology of man; attention must be paid to the prospects of change in the total social system if the 'ifs' are to be resolved. Attempts to change society by only changing education are, at best, somewhat naive; at worst they are a deception or a distraction in that, by focusing attention on the education system they allow the rest of the social system to remain unexamined and untouched. Either way they are almost certainly as questionable as the more extreme claims for ecological study, such as those of Nicholson (1970):

Ecology is the study of plants and animals in relation to their environment and to one another. But it is also more than that: it is the main intellectual discipline and tool which enables us to hope that human evolution can be mutated, can be shifted on to a new course, so that man will cease to knock hell out of the environment on which his own future depends.

115

Ecology and power

Yet the prevalence of naivety or even distortion in the consideration of the ecology of schooling need not cause us excessive depression. The evidence of this book shows that education unquestionably matters. Though an interdependent part of human ecology, it is a crucial element in maintaining the social system. And there is evidence from the more sophisticated work that has sprung from the Educational Priority project and similar endeavours that careful, detailed work can at least eliminate some of the inconsistencies and injustices within the present systems, and that resource distribution can compensate for resource deficiency and even redress conditions of marked inequality.

Perhaps above all there is a clear indication throughout the volume that a better understanding of the ecosystem is not only possible – and this book constitutes a contribution to it – but also that the understanding can allow actors in the ecosystem to engage in more informed and more effective behaviour within it. Above all it holds out the promise of being able to identify and participate in the exercise of power in a democratic society more adequately. Some of the most encouraging consequences of the new resource based curricula in the schools are that they not only alert students to the realities of the ecosystem but also give them the confidence and fluency to take part in decision making activity – contracting into the social system rather than being on its receiving end.

It is perhaps this prospect of active participation rather than passive interaction that holds out the greatest promise for the better working of the present ecosystem and the safest prelude to any attempts to modify it in the future. Only through their impact on consciousness can educational resources lead to an effective attack on the inequalities of the human condition.

References and name index

The numbers in italics after each entry refer to page numbers within this book.

Argyll Commission (1869) *Report of the Royal Commission on Schools in Scotland.* Edinburgh: HMSO *25*

Armitage, P. and Williams, G. (1976) *Planning Models in Education.* Milton Keynes: Open University Press. *27*

Ashby, E. (1975) The danger is political not ecological collapse. *Times Higher Educational Supplement* (19 December).

Averech, H. *et al.* (1972) *How Effective is Schooling? A Critical Review and Synthesis of Research Findings.* Santa Monica: The Rand Corporation. *62*

Barber, C. R. (1968) *A Follow up of School Leavers in Oxford City. Occasional Papers II.* Oxford: College of Technology Social Science Research Unit. *46*

Barker, R. G. and Gump, P. V. (1964) *Big School, Small School.* Stanfield, Calif.: University Press. *57*

Barnard, G. A., McCreath, M. and Freeman, J. (1967) *Notes on the Influence of the School Curriculum on the Flow of Pupils into Higher Education, Particularly the Universities.* Essex: The University. *109*

Barnes, J. H. (1977) Social mix and schooling. In Gleeson, D. (ed.) *Identity and Structure*. Driffield: Nafferton Books. *61*

Baron, G. and Howell, D. A. (1968) *School Management and Government Research Studies No. 6: Royal Commission on Local Government in England*. London: HMSO. *73*

Belding, R. and Hutchison, D. (1956) *Home or Away: Why Do Qualified Scottish School Leavers Move Away from Home?* Edinburgh: Centre for Educational Sociology, The University (mimeo). *38*

Benn, C. and Simon, B. (1970) *Half-Way There*. London: McGraw-Hill. *56*

Bernbaum, G. (1967) *Social Change and the Schools 1918–1944*. London: Routledge and Kegan Paul. *69*

Bernstein, B. (1970) A critique of the concept of compensatory education. In Rubenstein, D. and Stoneman, C. (eds) *Education for Democracy*. Harmondsworth: Penguin. *21*

Bernstein, B. (1971) On the classification and framing of educational knowledge. In Young, M. F. D. (ed.) *Knowledge and Control*. London: Collier–Macmillan. *95*

Bernstein, B. and Young, D. (1967) Social class differences in the use of toys. *Sociology 1*, 2. *61*

Blaug, M. (1970) *An Introduction to the Economics of Education*. London: Penguin. *20*

Boudon, R. (1973) *L'Inégalité des Chances*. Paris: Libraire Armand. *63*

Bowles, S. and Gintis, H. (1977) *Schooling in Capitalist America*. London: Routledge and Kegan Paul. *41, 63, 96, 114*

Boyle, E. (1967) *Conservatives and Economic Planning*. London: Conservative Political Centre. *26*

Boyle, E., Crosland, A. and Kogan, M. (1971) *The Politics of Education*. Harmondsworth: Penguin. *70, 71*

Brandis, W. and Henderson, D. (1970) *Social Class, Language and Communication*. London: Routledge and Kegan Paul.

Briault, E. (1974) *Allocation and Management of School Resources*. London: Council for Educational Technology. *73, 92–3*

Broady, M. (1967) Social theory and the planners. *New Society* (16 February), 232–4. *21*

Bullock Committee (1975) *A Language for Life*. London: HMSO. *70*

Byrne, D. and Williamson, B. (1972) Some intra-regional variations in educational provision and their bearing on educational attainment: the case of the North East. *Sociology 6*, 1. *38, 79–80*

Byrne, D., Williamson, B. and Fletcher, B. (1975) *The Poverty of Education*. London: Martin Robertson. *31–3, 43, 47, 48, 50–2, 56–7, 63–4*

Byrne, E. M. (1974) *Planning and Educational Inequality.* Slough: National Foundation for Educational Research. *73*

Byrne, E. M. (1976) *The Rationale of Resource Allocation.* Milton Keynes: Open University Press. *54, 68, 86–7*

Cicirellie, V. G. *et al.* (1969) *The Impact of Head Start on Children's Cognitive and Affective Development.* Washington: Westinghouse Learning Corporation (mimeo). *57*

Cicourel, A. V. and Kitsuse, J. I. (1963) *The Educational Decision Makers.* New York: Bobbs-Merrill. *109*

Coleman, J. S. (1966) *Equality of Educational Opportunity.* Washington: US Department of Health, Education and Welfare. *20, 56*

Crossman, R. S. H. (1975, 1976) *Diaries of a Cabinet Minister,* Vols 1 and 2. London: Hamish Hamilton. *70*

Crauzaz, R. (1974) *Diversification of Tertiary Education.* Strasbourg: Council of Europe. *20*

David, M. (1976) *Size and Education.* Bristol: Department of Social Administration, The University (mimeo). *55–6*

Donnison, D. V. and Chapman, B. (1965) *Social Policy and Administration.* London: Allen and Unwin. *74–5*

Douglas, J. W. B. (1964) *The Home and the School.* London: MacGibbon and Kee. *23*

Dutch Ministry of Education and Science (1975) *Contours of a Future Education System in the Netherlands.* The Hague: The Ministry. *20*

Eggleston, J. (1969) The social context of administration. In Baron, G. and Taylor, W. (eds) *Educational Administration and the Social Sciences.* London: Athlone.

Eggleston, J. (1973) Decision making in the school curriculum: a conflict model. *Sociology 7, 3. 95*

Eggleston, J. (1974a) Some environmental correlates of extended secondary education in England. In Eggleston, J. (ed.) *Contemporary Research in the Sociology of Education.* London: Methuen. *33–4, 46–9, 52–4*

Eggleston, J. (1974b) Going comprehensive. In Eggleston, J. (ed.) *Contemporary Research in the Sociology of Education.* London: Methuen. *74, 75*

Eggleston, J. (1976) *Adolescence and Community.* London: Edward Arnold. *110*

Eggleston, J. (1977) *The Sociology of the School Curriculum.* London: Routledge and Kegan Paul. *102*

Ford, J. (1968) *Social Class and the Comprehensive School*. London: Routledge and Kegan Paul. *97–8*

Glass, D. V. (ed.) (1954) *Social Mobility in Britain*. London: Routledge and Kegan Paul. *26*

Gould, R. (1976) The ecology of educational settings. *Educational Administration 4*, 2. *21, 105*

Gray, J. L. and Moshinsky, P. (1938) In Hogben, L. T. (ed.) *Political Arithmetic*. London: Gollancz. *26*

Halsey, A. H. (ed.) (1972) *Educational Priority*. London: HMSO. *25, 35–8, 43, 57–60*

Hargreaves, D. (1967) *Social Relations in a Secondary School*. London: Routledge and Kegan Paul. *78*

Hawkridge, D. G. *et al.* (1968) *A Study of Selected Exemplary Programs for the Education of Disadvantaged Children*. 2 Vols. Washington: US Department of Health, Education and Welfare. *57*

Hawley, A. H. (1950) *Human Ecology*. New York: Ronald Press. *17*

Hill, J. M. M. and Jacobs, M. S. (1976) *A Follow Up Study of Leavers from a London Comprehensive School*. London: Tavistock Institute of Human Relations.

Hoyle, E. (1975) Leadership and decision making in education. In Hughes, M. G. (ed.) *Administering Education: International Challenge*. London: Athlone.

Hutchison, D. (1975) Areas of difference: a critique of the work of Byrne and Williamson on regional inequalities in educational attainment. *Quality and Quantity 9*, 171–83. *38, 52*

Jackson, B. and Marsden, D. (1962) *Education and the Working Class*. London: Routledge and Kegan Paul. *39–40*

Jencks, C. (1972) *Inequality: A Reassessment of the Effect of Family and Schooling in America*. London: Allen Lane. *20, 43, 56, 62–3*

Jennings, R. E. (1976) *Interest Groups in English Local Education*. New York: State University at Buffalo (mimeo). *82, 83*

Jennings, R. E. (1977) *Politics and Policy Making in Local Education Authorities*. London: Batsford. *73*

Kimber, R. and Richardson, J. J. (eds) (1974) *Pressure Groups in Britain*. London: Dent. *80*

King, R. (1974) Short-course neighbourhood comprehensive schools: an LEA case study. *Educational Review 26*, 2. *61*

Kogan, M. (1975) *Educational Policy Making*. London: Allen and Unwin. *66, 69*

Kogan, M. and Packwood, T. (1974) *Advisory Councils and Committees in Education*. London: Routledge and Kegan Paul.

Lacey, C. (1970) *Hightown Grammar*. Manchester: University Press. *96*

Little, A. and Westergaard, J. (1964) The trend of class differentials in educational opportunity in England and Wales. *British Journal of Sociology 15*, 4. *63*

Lowe, P. D. and Worboys, M. R. (1975) *Ecology and Ideology*. Department of Sociology, Sheffield Polytechnic (unpublished mimeo). *17, 19, 114*

McHale, J. (1971) *The Ecological Context*. London: Studio Vista. *18*

Mclure, S. (1974) *Learning Beyond our Means?* London: Councils and Education Press. *86–7*

Meadows, D. H. *et al.* (1972) *The Limits to Growth*. New York: Earth Island. *17*

Midwinter, E. (1974) *Priority Education*. Harmondsworth: Penguin. *58*

Minar, D. W. (1966) *Education and Decision Making in Suburban Communities*. Evanston: North Western University Press. *72*

Monks, T. G. (ed.) (1970) *Comprehensive Education in Action*. Slough: NFER. *56*

Mood, A. M. (1967) On some basic steps in the application of systems analysis to instruction. *Socio-economic Planning Sciences 1*: 19–26. *76*

Myers, C. L. (1969) Operational research in educational administration. In Baron, G. and Taylor, W. (eds) *Educational Administration and the Social Sciences*. London: Athlone Press. *27*

Neave, G. (1975) *How They Fared*. London: Routledge and Kegan Paul. *34, 46, 107–9*

Newsom Report (1963) *Half Our Future*. London: HMSO. *28*

Nicholas, L. N. *et al.* (1965) *Effects of Socio-Economic Setting and Organizational Climate*. Detroit: Wayne State University Press. *72*

Nicholson, M. (1970) *The Environmental Revolution*. London: Hodder and Stoughton. *115*

Nicholson, S. (1972) The theory of loose parts. *Studies in Design Education and Craft 4*, 2. *21, 107*

Oates, J. (1974) *People in Cities*. Milton Keynes: Open University Press.

O'Riordan, T. (1971) *Perspectives in Resource Management.* London: Dion. *18*

Owen, J. G. (1975) Educational administration in England and Wales: the main issues. In Hughes, M. G. (ed.) *Administering Education: Internal Challenge.* London: Athlone.

Peaker, G. F. (1967) The Regression analysis of the national survey. In Plowden Report, *Children and their Primary Schools,* vol. 2. London: HMSO. *26, 51*

Plowden Report (1967) *Children and their Primary Schools,* vols. 1 and 2. London: HMSO. *24–5*

Poster, C. D. (1971) *The School and the Community.* London: Macmillan. *58*

Pratt, J., Burgess, T., Allemano, R. and Locke, M. (1973) *Your Local Education.* Harmondsworth: Penguin. *26, 31, 44, 46*

Pyle, D. J. (1975) Intra-regional variations in educational provision . . . some comments on Byrne and Williamson. *Sociology 9,* 3. *52*

Quinn, J. A. (1964) Ecology. In Gould, J. (ed.) *Dictionary of the Social Sciences.* London: Tavistock. *17*

Richardson, E. (1967) *The Environment of Learning: Conflict and Understanding in the Secondary School.* London: Nelson *21, 106*

Robbins Report (1963) *Higher Education.* London: HMSO. *24*

Robinson, P. (1976) *Education and Poverty.* London: Methuen. *35, 59*

Rogoff, N. (1961) Local social structure and educational selection. In Halsey, A. H., Floud, J. and Anderson, C. A. (eds) *Education, Economy and Society.* Glencoe: Free Press. *40*

Roy, W. (1974) Membership participation in the National Union of Teachers. In Kimber, R. and Richardson, J. J. (eds) *Pressure Groups in Britain.* London: Dent. *80*

Saran, R. (1973) *Policy Making in Secondary Education.* Oxford: Clarendon Press. *73, 75*

Schools Council (1968) *Enquiry 1. Young School Leavers.* London: HMSO. *107*

Schutz, A. (1967) Choosing among projects of action. In Schutz, A., *Collected Papers, 1: The Problems of Social Reality.* The Hague: Nijhoff. *112–13*

Sharp, R. and Green, A. (1975) *Education and Social Control.* London: Routledge and Kegan Paul. *98–100, 114*

Shipman, M. D., Bolam, D. and Jenkins, D. (1974) *Inside a Curriculum Project.* London: Methuen. *100*

Steele, F. (1973) *Physical Settings and Organization Development.*
  Reading, Mass: Addison-Wesley. *103*
Stone, R. (1965) A model of the education system. *Minerva 3.* *76*
Stone, R. (1966) Input/output and demographic accounting:
  A tool for educational planning. *Minerva 4.* *76*

Taylor, G. and Ayres, N. (1969) *Born and Bred Unequal.* London:
  Longmans. *26, 27–8, 29–30, 43, 44, 46*
Taylor, W. (1963) *The Secondary Modern School.* London: Faber
  and Faber. *108*
Tyler, W. (1977) *The Sociology of Educational Inequality.* London:
  Methuen. *62*

Vaizey, J. (1963) *The Control of Education.* London: Faber and
  Faber. *69.*
Vaizey, J. and Sheehan, J. (1968) *Resources for Education.* London:
  Allen and Unwin. *66*
Vaughan, M. and Archer, M. S. (1971) *Social Conflict and Educa-
  tional Change in England and France 1789–1848.* Cambridge:
  University Press. *95*

Wax, M. L. and Wax, R. H. (1964) Formal education in an Ameri-
  can Indian community. *Social Problems Monographs* No. 2. *99*
Weinberg, A. (1969) Education. In Stacey, C. (ed.) *Comparability
  in Social Research.* London: Heinemann. *45*
Wiseman, S. (1964) *Education and Environment.* Manchester:
  University Press. *26*

Schramm, W. (1964) Mass Media and Development in Developing Countries. Reading, Mass: Addison-Wesley. 103

Stacey, J. (1969) A model of the education system, Milano. 49

Stone, R. (1966) Demographic and demographic accounting and its relation for educational planning. New York. 70

Taylor, G. and Ayres, N. (1969) Born and Bred Unequal. London: Longmans. 39, 52, 79, 82

Tucker, J. (1962) The Spanning Matrix School. London: Pitman. 138

Turner, W. (1977) The Education and Training Support in London. Methuen. 72

Vaizey, K. (1960) The theory of educational discussion. Paper ... 67

Vaizey, John, Sheehan, J. (1968) Resources for Education. London: Allen and Unwin. 66

Vaughan, M. and Archer, M. S. (1971) Social conflict and Educational Change in England and France 1780–1848. Cambridge: University Press. 17

Webb, Sidney and Webb, B. H. (1920) Industrial democracy in all Modern Trades Unionism. Social Democracy. Manchester. 70

Woodhall, A. (1972) Economics of Education, Cost-benefit in School Finance. London: Heinemann. 53

Vreeman, R. (1968) Education and Environment. London: University Press. 20

Subject index

125